TWO AND A HALF

NICKLES

TWO AND A HALF

NICKLES

DONALD S. BURNS

authorHOUSE®

AuthorHouse™
1663 Liberty Drive
Bloomington, IN 47403
www.authorhouse.com
Phone: 1-800-839-8640

First published by AuthorHouse   01/27/2012

ISBN: 978-1-4685-4724-5 (sc)
ISBN: 978-1-4685-4723-8 (hc)
ISBN: 978-1-4685-4173-1 (ebk)

Library of Congress Control Number: 2012901408

Printed in the United States of America

CONTENTS

CHAPTER ONE

When does an adventure start?
Is it in the wee hours of the morning when sleep becomes an elusive demon darting from your grasp? Or is it at a cocktail party when you're nakedly revealing your dreams of visiting with a sensuous half-dressed Polynesian girl on the island of Bora-Bora?

I can't really pin down just when our adventure started, but I know it was long before I signed the charter agreement for the M.Y. *Cuhona* and made airplane and hotel reservations for the ten of us.

In my case, I believe my adventure started the night that . . .

"Luke, I'm fed up with the whole ball of wax. I've lost rapport with people in the company, I've collected my profit sharing, and I'm as nervous as a cat on the proverbial roof, so I've decided to chuck the whole damn mess. Today I'm a man. I resigned. Yep, I told them to shove it in their ear."

"Honey, I'm with you the whole route. Now what are you going to do?" was her agreeable reply.

"Well, I'm not just exactly sure, but now that we've got two and a half nickels to rub together, let's take the kids to Europe and spend a year spending. Since I'll be broke when I get back, I'm really going to enjoy myself before I have to buckle down again. I know I can get a good job to rebuild our finances, so what the hell, are you with me?"

"I'm ahead of you, dear. Let's call the kids at school in Arizona and give them the news."

"Okay. You tell those three, and I'll break the news to the group here."

I think that was the genesis of our adventure.

My eager and fun-loving wife, Lucy—Luke to me and her intimates—really pushed the go button by her immediate acceptance of my dream. The telephone call to our three oldest gals in school

1

added even more fuel to the blast. The three gals at home were perhaps somewhat less enthusiastic, especially Robin, age three, who flatly refused to go unless she could take her "blankie."

Yes, I had committed myself right up to my eyeballs, and I hoped no one would go by in a motorboat to upset our dreams.

The prospects were even brighter after Luke and I made a preliminary trip to Switzerland in February 1966 to look for schools for all six children. The fact that we spent more than half our time looking for new and unspoiled ski areas did not deter us from our school search. As a matter of fact, we were highly successful in locating schools in Switzerland and disposing of each of our big and little demons in various well-watched, well-chaperoned institutions for *les jeunes filles*. That's not what the evil-minded reader might think—that's a girls' school.

Julie, eighteen and our oldest, a high school graduate who had been accepted at Stanford University in Palo Alto, received a year's deferment and was entered at the Institut Richelieu in Lausanne. There she was to specialize in French and take various other courses in boy watching, business, and the avoidance of the continental pinch, a favorite sport for us old-time continentals.

Patti, sixteen, and Laurie, fifteen, were accepted at a wonderful school in Gstaad, the Institut Montesano. Here the girls specialize in skiing, French, skiing, and as a minor subject, boys.

Wendi, our thirteen-year-old, was to attend Brillantmont, an outstanding girls' school in Lausanne. Here there is no fun in the sun other than highly supervised activities along with a very challenging academic program. To my knowledge, Brillantmont is the only fully accredited school to Stanford in Switzerland.

We had planned to send Lonnie, our eleven-year-old, to Montjoie in Villars s. Ollon, but a change in plans that I will divulge later in this narrative prevented her attendance.

Our crew was rounded out by three-year-old Robin, blanket on one shoulder and thumb in mouth, along with her close friend Chris Karl, twenty-one-year-old glorified babysitter, nurse, student of skiing, sailing, and more particularly, student of life.

"You're out of your cotton-pickin' head" was the spoken consensus of our Newport Beach friends.

"You'll go out of that pinhead of yours traveling with all that girl-type company," commented many of my business associates.

"You won't last ten weeks" was the caustic comment of my faithful and forever enduring secretary.

For that matter, everyone with an encouraging comment such as the foregoing was right!

But that's getting ahead of myself and ruining the supposed suspense that I am trying to build in order to make this story a saleable commodity. After all, if I can peddle this to some unsuspecting editor, I can write off the expense of the adventure.

CHAPTER TWO

M y experience in the planning of this grand adventure has proved, beyond that dimly lit shadow called doubt, that the best-laid plans of mice and men too often get all fouled up.

Once the aura of wonderment of realizing that we were really going ahead with this trip had subsided, some of the stark realities of how, when, where, and who bubbled to the surface. These so-called facts had a slight effect in tempering the enjoyment of anticipation, but when you've got your neck out, it has to be full throttle ahead.

We wavered considerably on what to do during the summer, fall, and spring months. Winter was no problem because we knew that skiing and stretch-pants-watching would keep me busy. We thought that the best thing to do was to put our beautiful fifty-three-foot, Garden-designed ketch, *Little Revenge,* on the market for sale or for an annual charter. Then we would use some of the fabulous charter income or large profit from the sale to help us finance the charter of such a boat as the hundred-foot, American-owned ketch, the *Kikki.*

After much discussion with the yacht brokers here in the West and a few in the East, I signed the listings and put my dear love on the auction block. There was no real need for concern, because after the initial pitch by the brokers, nothing happened. I guess the stock market went sour, or the real estate market was bad, but no eager large-boat bidders appeared fully rigged with a bone in their teeth. As a matter of fact, we didn't see even one hull down on the horizon.

Correspondence started to flow back and forth over the Atlantic and into the far reaches and corners of the Mediterranean. It was our intention to charter, or perhaps even buy, a cruising ketch in European waters for our cruise, which would occupy the summer, fall, and spring. These letters instituted the first pall of discouragement.

Boats that were older, smaller, less well equipped, and rather ratty in appearance were available at only twice the price that we were asking for our beautiful, fully equipped, modern, and immaculate *Little Revenge*.

It was obvious that we were walking into a dark den of slick pirates who were out to scalp the rich, jet-set Americans. Frankly, true blue discouragement set in. We were getting buyer's remorse. We began to figure out the daily budget, and after multiplying our daily figure by 365, we found that this astronomical sum was really going to dissipate the estate that I had spent twenty years trying to build.

The only thing that prevented me from swallowing my pride and calling the whole thing off was that when I pussyfooted around the subject with the kids and Luke, I received icy looks and reproachful stares. I just didn't have the guts to back out then.

Unhappily, there was no activity on either a bona fide charter or the sale of the *Little Revenge*. I did have some wheelers and dealers make me all sorts of indecent propositions, such as running the boat as a floating house of ill repute. They would split fifty/fifty on the take and even offered me free guest privileges. Other people offered to "take care" of the *Little Revenge* while I was away for a year. I even was offered a deal whereby I paid the expenses of a group of mixed single protesters to go to the South Pacific, where they were planning to protest the French hydrogen bomb test. This group assured me that they were nonprofit and that therefore all the expenses, including depreciation, would be tax deductible.

There was a lull developing in our plan—and decision-making progress. Many future contingencies started to revolve around when or if we could charter the *Little Revenge*. Even the yacht brokers were ominously quiet after their rash of usual promises. Then I started to have some sleepless nights wondering what I was to do with my little beauty, the *Little Revenge*.

While cruising to Catalina Island one weekend on a beautiful balmy day with a force 3 wind, Luke remarked how wonderful it would be to have our own boat, which we knew and trusted so well, with us in the Mediterranean. The idea nestled comfortably in the back of my mind, and as we cut through the waters of the blue Pacific under almost cloudy skies, I imagined this to be the same exhilarating experience I would enjoy while slipping along the sunlit shores of Costa Brava.

By the time we pulled into White's Landing on Catalina, I expected the Spanish port authorities to bustle out to the *Little Revenge* and ask for our clearance papers. The spell was broken when one of my neighbors yelled over a greeting and an invitation to cocktails as soon as the sun got anywhere near the yardarm. The idea, however, was not lost. As a matter of fact, I began to like it more and more.

There was an actual bedlam of enthusiastic assent when I mentioned it to the gals that same evening. I admit my thoughts may have been stimulated by the wholesome and delicious dinner that Luke had just prepared in our galley. The delightful Rhein-Hassen wine that we had with our gourmet dinner didn't hurt either.

As we adjourned to the cockpit to look at the brilliant orange and red of the setting sun, I lost myself once more to the future. This was the only way a man should go . . . with his own boat, his wonderful family, enjoying the advantages of beautiful foreign shores . . . Maybe tomorrow there would be some of the cute little bikini-clad Spanish girls to look at through my binoculars . . . Man, this is living . . .

"Hey . . . Don," bellowed a voice, "come on over for an after-dinner drink . . . You asleep or something?"

Gone were the bikinis, back came White's Landing. We were being boarded not by customs officials, but by some of the gang from the yacht club. I had to tuck my dreams away until I could get rid of these unappreciative, overzealous Americans.

Soon after returning from that three-day cruise I called my secretary into my office and said, "Lynchie, find out what ships could carry the *Little Revenge* to Barcelona."

"Don, do you feel all right?" she queried.

"Don't question the boss—hop to it. I want a report tomorrow morning with shipping schedules and prices."

Lynchie left with a look on her face that said the boss had popped his cotton-pickin' head. Resigned to the inevitability of the command, she started warming up the telephone lines to Los Angeles. At eight thirty the next morning she placed before me the schedule of times and prices with other information such as insurance costs during shipping and while cruising in Europe, cradle costs, and so on. She had done an excellent, thorough job. The total cost staggered me. I tucked the information into my desk, feeling that if I didn't look at it for a while, it might be possible for me to rationalize this huge expenditure before

I had to break the news to Luke. How does one go about rationalizing a twelve-thousand-dollar cost—one way! Hell, I'd said her back from Europe. Thus began my train of thought so I could sell this program to Luke.

That evening between the day-end activities and the before-supper rush, I poured Luke a good stiff vodka martini and fortified myself with a fine French aperitif.

"You know, honey, those boats we saw in Europe were really pretty filthy. Further, I'm sure a foreign crew would take advantage of our good nature and easygoing ways. All in all, the only real answer to our problem is to take the *Little Revenge* with us.

"I found out we can ship her via the Italpacific Lines and in twenty-eight days have her offloaded in Barcelona. There she can be re-rigged, have a quick bottom and topside job—and we'd have our own boat, our own crew, and our own comforts available when we struck out on our adventure into the blue seas of the Mediterranean."

"How much is this going to set us back?" was her first question, which was immediately followed by, "Are you going to send over our own skipper?" A torrent of other questions followed.

"Hey, slow down!" was the only defensive remark I could make. "Take it easy and I'll try to answer one question at a time. Here . . . have another martini."

I don't know whether the extra one or two martinis or my persuasive, almost desperate sales appeal turned the trick, but before supper we both agreed that even though it might cost us more than the two and a half nickels we had saved, we should send the *Little Revenge* to Spain. Easy come, easy go—except that the easy-go seemed much easier than the easy-come.

Again, the routine of planning the details took over our activities. Negotiations with the shipping lines became intense, and I attempted to get a special rate. The insurance company was asked to take a closer look at their figures, and I commenced looking for competitive prices on all aspects of our expenses . . . tourist versus family rates on the airlines, first class rather than deluxe hotels, shipment of American staples aboard the *Little Revenge*, and other corner-cutting devices were beginning to fall in line. It appeared that sagacious savings could be made if we were willing to sacrifice just a little comfort. I should put this more strongly: we had to sacrifice to save.

Our spirits were elevating again. Planning became a period of fun-filled anticipation. We started to read all the available literature on various potential ports of visitation. We studied Field and Fodor's. The former seemed to approach these tourist traps with a wonderful tongue-in-cheek humor. The latter lacked the comedy, but appeared to be more cognizant of the "two and a half nickel" problem. Amazingly, we found very little literature available on a pure cruising guide. For some reason the people who have cruised extensively in the Mediterranean are more interested in reporting on the wealth of history than divulging the best way to approach that special rock-rimmed bay that houses a truly safe and peaceful anchorage.

The building blocks were falling into place and the adventure seemed a sure shot.

It looked like we were ready to go . . .

CHAPTER THREE

The strongest structure, if shaken hard enough, can come tumbling down. Even though the bricks that went into building our plans seemed to be well laid, the whole thing was toppled by a single telephone conversation.

I was at my desk one afternoon when a business associate called.

"Don, would you be interested in going ahead with that dealership we discussed almost a year ago, if we raised the allocation, made the concessions you asked for at that time, and changed the location to be within ten miles of Newport Beach?"

"Yes" I replied without hesitation.

There, in one word, I had blown the adventure of a lifetime.

How was I going to break the news to the troops? I sort of felt trapped between pleasure and opportunity, memories and money, or perhaps stupidity and shrewdness.

The *yes* I had just given to the business opportunity was irrevocable. Now I had to go home and sell this new concept to the troops.

I stayed in the office quite late that evening, mainly because I was afraid to break the news. I knew Luke and the kids were counting on the program we had previously planned. I figured that when one got stuck in a situation like this, the best thing to do was compromise. With that thought in mind I carefully drew plans that would allow, I hoped, everyone to enjoy part of what we had anticipated.

When all was written down and organized, I left the sanctuary of my office and was prepared to enter the den of lionesses. If I'd been a drinking man, I would have stopped at the famous sternwheeler, the Reuben E. Lee, for liquid fortification and professional sympathy from my friends—but damn me troubles, full speed to the barn.

"Hi, Luke, what's new?" I queried just to avoid temporarily the inevitable. I listened to the outline of her day and felt guilty listening to her humdrum existence. No wonder she was looking forward to our now shattered adventure.

"And how did your day go, Don? Anything new at the office?"

With a now-or-never approach, I plunged in.

"Our year's trip is off. I made a deal to open a new automobile agency near here. But I've got it figured out that we can spend two or three months in Europe this summer cruising the Adriatic, the Mediterranean, or the Agean.

"Any of the kids who want to go to school in Switzerland can do so. Don't get upset—everything is not lost . . . I'll make it up to all of you in some way."

I shuddered to a halt and prepared for the counterattack.

"That's all right, dear. We can do anything you think is best. I'll tell the gang in Arizona if you'll take care of the other arrangements."

Dread is 90 percent anticipation as is, on the opposite end of the scale, the pleasure connected with anticipation. I had just shed myself of the mangle of dread, and now I looked forward with eagerness I did not expect to rehashing all the plans we had laboriously made.

We decided to let all the school arrangements for the four oldest girls stand. Lonnie, our number five, decided she did not want to tackle a new school, a foreign language, and strange customs all in one gulp and asked to be able to matriculate here in the States.

Telephone calls were made to cancel the shipping arrangements and insurance on the *Little Revenge*. The man building the cradle was stopped just in the nick of time before he laid a saw to the lumber. I did have to pay for the blueprints and design of the cradle, but I've tucked them away for future reference.

I would like to express my sincere appreciation to Mr. William Garden, designer of the *Little Revenge*. Bill Garden did not design the boat for me and was under no obligation to furnish the information he did. By phone and by letter I took up a great deal of this man's time, and not once did he even suggest any remuneration. When I broached the subject, he indicated that he was doing it for the pleasure of helping an adventurous yachtsman. With men like that, how can we boat owners go wrong?

Everything was unraveled with practically nonsnarls except perhaps some justifiable resentment on behalf of the shipping lines. They had

had a pigeon almost on the spit, and I suspect they're still wondering how and why I got away.

The undoing was relatively easy, but the nagging question haunted us as to what now. Frankly, I only had the vague and haunting notion that if I wanted to keep my happy family happy, I'd better get off the dime and start generating a brilliantly conceived plan of action.

Somehow, however, it just didn't seem to come together. I felt like an athlete who had run his best race in the elimination events. Around the house there was a deafening silence. A few furtive questions would be directed my way about when and where our proposed grand tour would go. I could only growl some unintelligible answer to the effect that I was working on it and "for Christ's sake, quit buggin' me!" Regardless of how I prodded myself and despite the halfhearted attempts I made to create something, I just seemed to draw zero. All the old salts supposedly say, "It's always darkest before the dawn," and I agree. There was no light flickering anywhere in the future.

"Don, we've been invited as John and Sunny Elliott's guests to see some pictures of a trip that Bill and Marcia Mae Bents took through the Mediterranean. Do you want to go?" quietly queried my ever patient wife.

"Sure, honey, maybe we'll get an inspiration" was my rather lame, frustrated reply.

My reply turned out to be the understatement of the year.

The dinner before the showing of the films was delicious. The company was stimulating inasmuch as half the Newport Beach yachting fraternity was on hand and many of my friends stirred my eagerness by discussing some of their voyages to the far reaches of the sea. The frosting on the cake was the excellent pictorial report of the Bents's cruise. The total effect was to put me back on a creative beam, but, more surprisingly and pleasing, the evening's inspiration built a full-blown bonfire under Luke, and she really picked up the ball and started to creatively construct the framework of our voyage-to-be.

The next day she called Marcia Mae and invited the Bents, along with other friends, to our home for dinner to discuss further the details of their trip. The dinner took place just a few evenings later and was an even greater stimulation than we expected. Bill and Marcia Mae were wonderful in unselfishly donating their time and information to help us plan our venture.

They gave us charts of their travels, their log chucked full of information, their address book, hotel lists, medical supply lists, food lists, and all sorts of varied and helpful data.

While Luke ferreted out the tidbits of intelligence that make a trip that much more enjoyable, I charged ahead making the financial, travel, charter, and accommodation plans. I cabled Mr. P. Strauss in Cannes asking him if the *Cuhona*, the eighty-three-foot diesel motor yacht the Bents had used on their trip, was available for charter. I received a cable the next day setting out the available dates. A letter went off that night and we elected to charter the *Cuhona* on August 3 for departure from Venice with final destination Piraeus, port of Athens, Greece.

Now I felt like a small Pentagon planning an overseas campaign. Don't kid yourself, launching an attack such as the ten of us planned was a major logistical problem.

You may wonder how our party grew to ten. A word of explanation is due. That word is boyfriends. Yes, our daughters have very persuasive talents in that they sold Luke and me the idea and their boyfriends the thought, and even more challengingly persuaded the parents of the boys to allow them to become part of our ragged but rugged crew. The boys were Tom Chauncey from Phoenix, our oldest daughter's friend, and Pete Niggeman from San Francisco, big brother to all the girls. Tom joined us in Los Angeles, and we met Pete, who had traveled to Europe ahead of us, in Venice.

Pan American Airlines should love me. I booked seats for nine of us departing on PAA Flight 120 at noon on July 25. We made arrangements to fly nonstop to London. We would change planes after a four-hour wait and then fly to Geneva. Our plans called for four days in Lausanne and then taking a train to Venice. All hotel reservations were made and confirmed. Trunks for the girls who would be remaining in Switzerland for the coming school year were purchased, packed, and sent on ahead. Clothes were bought, medical supplies were organized, and even Robin's blanket was cut down to a more convenient travel size.

On June 25 we put Patti, who wished to attend the American School in Switzerland Summer Program, on a plane for Europe. Our advanced guard was off. The show was all but on the road.

June 30 was my last day with Ekco, and after sixteen and a half years I became a statistic in the war on poverty. I had no visible means of support, but nothing bothered me. I had lots to look forward to, no regrets, and no qualms about the future.

I will admit that the money started to flow out of the coffers at an alarming rate. More than six thousand dollars for transportation. Seven grand went to Mr. Strauss for the charter of the *Cuhona*. Hotel deposits took a couple of hundred. Shoes, slacks, shirts, and stuff for all the troops nibbled at the fast-diminishing pile. We just had to adopt the attitude that we knew this was costing us a mint but it was all going to be worth it, and that pleasant memories are more valuable than big bank accounts and large tax payments to the government.

The intent of everyone's friends is to make a departure a thing of joy and pleasure. Each in turn desires to impress upon the impending voyager that parting is such sweet sorrow. In my case the parting parties resulted in a severe but fortunately not chronic case of posterior dragitis.

Starting a week before our getaway day we were invited nightly to close, intimate dinners at which humorous cards and trivia were bestowed on us. Frankly, as each gathering gave way to the next, more eagerness crept into my mind waiting for the coming event. I had to leave to survive the rigors of this nightly social life. It was even more of a problem for Luke because her lovely and vivacious girlfriends gave her liquid luncheons. One in particular flowed so freely that outside recruits had to be commandeered to drive the participants home. These fluid events resounded around the community to the extent that my secretary became involved and even her afternoons became rather vague approaches to the problem of getting my records and files in shape for my trip.

I knew with some finality that the great day was approaching when I packed my big black Labrador retriever, Diamond, into the car and drove her to Ed Asmus's training kennel. I felt that Diamond knew I was going away for some time, because she snuggled extra close to me after getting into the car. Her soulful look almost turned my heart and head into thinking I should take her with me. Upon arrival at the kennel she was on particularly good behavior. She showed off beautifully by obeying hand and whistle signals. I was quite proud of her performance in front of professional handlers. However, I hardened myself and turned her over to the attendant. I was about to leave when Ed Asmus asked me about my future hunting plans, and whether I planned to start a young pup to replace Diamond when she was ready to retire from hunting. After a short discussion he took me and two of my daughters, Laurie, my hunting companion, and Robin, the blanket addict, out back to look at some pups. Well, I'm here to say that I just didn't stand a chance. There were three pups in one cage, two-three months old. They were having a ball playing with one another. One was a black female, one a golden male, and one a chocolate male. All had good conformation and all were going to be of good size, but the golden caught my eye and buried himself in my heart. Not only did he have huge paws and a slick coat, but his antics of diving into the water bucket to retrieve flying leaves was so amusing that the extraction of his purchase price was absolutely painless.

The girls who were with me agreed with my decision, and we left the kennel full of the love of life and knowledge that we now owned two beautiful Labradors as well as two fine poodles.

As we turned into our street, the thought dawned on me that one more dog in the house was probably the last straw as far as Luke was concerned. Our joy was short lived, and it gave way to consternation and feverish plotting for ways to break the news. I have never claimed to be a hero, and because of my admitted reticence, Robin was elected to break the news.

Laurie and I carefully primed her, and when we felt she knew her lines, in the door she was shoved. She galloped to her mother's room yelling, "We've got Tops, he's beautiful, I love him, he's a golden Labrador—aren't you glad, Mommy?"

Mommy might not have been glad; after almost twenty years, she was used to her impulsive husband and greeted the news with a resigned sigh, commenting, "That's nice, isn't it?"

CHAPTER FOUR

Getaway day arrived with the faint first light of dawn. I knew that it was just too early to go leaping out of the sack, and besides I couldn't have leaped anywhere after the final round of going-away parties. I didn't have a hangover, but I had something akin to it that us nondrinkers get.

With no place to rush to, I lay abed wondering what I had yet to do, what we had forgotten, and what would happen if I decided to abort the mission. Wild, irrelevant thoughts rushed around my already muddled mind. I pondered the consequences of taking a sleeping pill now, it being 5:00 a.m. Will I sleep through the whole day? Will the rest of the group be able to rouse me? Do I have enough money? Will Diamond and the new pup be all right? Those nudist colonies in Yugoslavia must really be something. I had better purchase a pair of binoculars in Switzerland so I can report a close view to my curious Newport Beach friends.

"Let's go, Daddy. I'm all ready. My blanket is packed and Chris will be here right away" was the greeting Robin yelled in my ear. I bolted upright and whirled to look at my watch on the bedside stand. Wow, it was 7:30 a.m.—what had happened? I guess thinking of those lovely naked Slav beauties was a really great sleeping potion. However, Robin, in her lily-white underpants, was just the thing to bring me back to reality.

I glanced at Luke, and her reassuring smile and not-so-gentle shove finally got the old bones moving. After a leisurely shower and careful shave, I wandered to the breakfast table to find I wasn't the last one out of the sack. I had to roust Laurie out of her reveries. Maybe she was dreaming of the Slavs also, but, I hoped, from a different point of view.

Amazingly enough everything went quite well. Breakfast was finished, the house cleaned, the bags stowed in the car. We were ready to go and were still a half hour early. We fiddled and fussed. Luke loaded everyone with Marezine for motion sickness, and finally we piled into the car. Lynchie, ever faithful, arrived in her car to help with the transport. We stopped and picked up Nickie Crecca, who was to return our car to its garage. Believe it or not, we were under way—at least to the heliport.

Actually, all went very smoothly. The helicopter was on time and deposited us at the Los Angeles airport swiftly and without incident. As we trooped over to the inter-terminal bus, Luke was asked what tour group we were. We told the inquisitor that we were part of a circus act on our way to play the Palladium in London. The truth would have been even more absurd.

Our arrival at Pan American really shook up the young lady in charge of the Clipper Club. We were informed that each member was allowed only two guests. It looked for a while as though most of the troupe was going to be relegated to the corridor outside the club while I went inside and lushed up some easy living. I figured that type of segregation wasn't going to make for a very happy beginning, so I used my most severe and anguished tone of persuasion and after talking to the supervisor, moved all the crew inside to the lap of luxury. I must admit that once past this critical hurdle, our treatment was more in keeping with the vast fortune I had shoved Pan American's way. The supervisor on duty more than made up for the slight mix-up at the Clipper Club.

We were checked in with speed and efficiency, a row and a half of seats were set aside, and we were hustled aboard an absolutely full aircraft without any unnecessary problems. I was very grateful that Tom Chauncey had joined us in Los Angeles, because I gave him some hand luggage to carry.

I was amused by playing the game I've played over many years of travel. I call it People Watching. I pass the time wondering who they are, where they're going, and what they're going to do. I think it's a fascinating game and very easy to play. You make your own rules and play as long as you like. You can't cheat. I highly recommend it to all who travel. Of course if everyone played the game simultaneously, the place could look like an insane asylum . . . kooks looking at kooks.

One interesting example of People Watching took place just before our takeoff. Two obviously continental gentlemen with airs of experienced travelers were seated in two of three seats. They were conspiring to make sure the seat between them remained unoccupied. It looked as if they had it made until a Pan Am agent went through the plane looking for an empty seat. Despite the camouflage, the eagle-eyed agent spotted the available seat. The gentlemen were asked if they were traveling together. If not, a young, attractive mother and child would like to occupy two seats if one of the gentlemen would move. The conspirators quickly decided they were together and couldn't possibly be separated. The agent left. The newfound friends were joyous at the success of their skillful maneuver. They were so pleased at having outwitted the airlines that they failed to notice a rather old, fat, and unattractive lady waddling down the aisle in their direction. Without an aye, yes or no, she thrust her large bulk in one fast, gigantic heave and landed between Alphonse and Gaston.

There's a moral there somewhere, but I'm not sure what it was except that I love to see a smartass get outsmarted.

People Watching, although giving one a great sense of satisfaction, goes only so far. The flight itself was run-of-the mill average, smooth. The food contained two of the four standard airline menus. The usual boredom set in. Sleep finally overcame all of us, and I think I was dead to the world for a solid twenty minutes when it was announced we would land in Montreal for fuel. Since we had a four-hour layover in London to look forward to, we didn't mind wasting part of it in Montreal.

Unfortunately, they would not allow us off the aircraft, but at least we were granted the privilege of a breath of fresh Canadian air. Of course, you had to crawl, scratch, and claw your way through the mass of humanity jammed around the rear cabin door. I have to give Luke credit. She actually made it to the top of the ramp with Robin in her arms. Oh well, a lady with a baby can get away with most anything.

Departure from Montreal put us smack into the middle of a large frontal activity. There was lightning all around, above, below, port, and starboard. The plane careened from one bump to the next. If you've ever seen a cabin full of white-knuckle fliers, you know exactly what we experienced. Fortunately, the Marezine did its work and our crew survived without even a burp. Cribbage, gin rummy, and poker occupied the remaining hours as we jetted the Atlantic.

Arrival in London was two hours late, but the tardiness was of no concern to us. We had much time and little to do. Coffee and rolls became uppermost in our minds. Robin even forgot her blanket for a moment and concentrated on her desire for a glass of milk. At first we were frustrated in our search. We wandered around the departure terminal and could find only long lines of harried and hurried travelers waiting to have some sort of nourishment thrown at them from across a counter by equally harried and hurried attendants.

Those lines were just too long for me, and I thought I might have to ignore the pleas for nourishment from my starving crew. Mutiny was rumbling low in their stomachs. The situation was not quite at the desperation point, but the signs were ominous. The luck of the Irish prevailed, and by chance I stumbled into a very small, out-of-the-way coffee and tea shop. For those who come after us, this shop is between the transfer check-in lounge and the departure lounge. Don't rush or you'll go right by the entrance.

We were attended by a most delightful English lady who had an early-morning twinkle in her eye and a delightful, bright sense of humor to match. When I told her I didn't have English money to use as payment, she replied with eyes agleam that she was like any woman and would take any kind of money at any time. This lovely lady then proceeded to tell me how lucky I was to have such a grand family. Needless to add, I overtipped in typical American fashion.

The English airlines, and particularly British European Airways, learned a lesson well from the invasion of the friendly American forces during World War II: the old army rule of "hurry up and wait awhile."

We were called to our plane for the last flying leg of our journey forty minutes before flight time. This call to embark seemed urgent, as if departure were imminent and even ahead of schedule. I should have known better from past experience. However, we did well in that we were only thirty-five minutes behind schedule in leaving. All was not black, because we had excellent tail winds and made up some of the time with a flight of less than an hour to Geneva.

Being an amateur pilot and having flown a few jets myself, I have to admit I still get egg-size goose pimples when flying with the RAF type. I can't get used to having these very skilled pilots reverse engines in the air while still forty to fifty feet above the ground. It just scares the hell out of me. Needless to add, it's their technique, it works—and they're welcome to it.

Swiss customs officials are really great. They look you in the eye and ask if you're a smuggler. If you said yes, they'd be so surprised that they'd let you go just as a reward for not lying. They must have ESP because they didn't bother any one of the seventy to eighty passengers on our flight. As a matter of fact, they never have examined a suitcase in the ten or twelve times I've entered their wonderful country. In the United States I've come through customs more than twenty times, and each time I've had to bare my dirty underwear and messy clothes to all my fellow passengers, who look upon them with disdain. Someday I'm going to return to the States with all clean clothes, neatly arranged in impeccable order just to impress everyone. That's the day I'll probably get the smile of welcome and a wave of the official hand to pass without inspection.

We all made it without incident and collected our seventeen pieces of luggage. I couldn't quite see myself trying to organize an army of stevedores to load our baggage on a bus, from the bus to a train, from a train to taxis, and from taxis to the hotel. I think I did it the cheap way.

I hired two of the "we try harder" best Volkswagen Variant squareback sedans, the world's greatest. The "Number Two" really went out of their way in helping, even to loading our bags, holding Robin, and all but kissing us goodbye as they wished us on to the road to Lausanne.

The drive to Lausanne from Geneva is usually a breeze, but I was so beat, I could hardly stay awake and had to sing in my usual liltingly off-key, flat voice to keep myself on the ball. My singing is so bad that absolutely no one could sleep through it. In this manner we narrowly escaped running off the superhighway from Geneva to Lausanne.

Once in Lausanne I had to unlimber my rusty French so as to ask directions to our hotel. I had to inquire only four times and made only three wrong turns. Lausanne is very confusing to the neophyte inasmuch as there is no pattern or orderliness to the streets. They were all laid out by Swiss cows a thousand years before the automobile, and I must add that even the cows wouldn't make it today.

Arrival at the Hotel Montana looked like an invasion of weary, worried, and overworked prospectors. We were prospecting, all right. We were looking for a much desired and needed rest. Our search was well rewarded because the rooms, beds, and service were great. The only slight deterrent was that the guests were all very elderly. As one of the kids put it, "This hotel is where the old folks go to visit their grandparents." I assure you this atmosphere of older folks discouraged us not. The price of these excellent accommodations would have induced me to bunk in with Methuselah himself.

And so to sleep. We had arrived!

CHAPTER FIVE

A good rest, a warm shower, and clean clothes made for a new Burns family. We all arrived down in the lobby of the Hotel Montana beaming with energy, ready to tackle further exploratory adventures. The only problem was that it was nine o'clock at night. Robin couldn't understand why it was not sunny when she got up from her sleep. I started to try to explain, but quickly gave up, knowing that it was going to get much too involved for my simple mind.

Even though we had just arisen, we made arrangements to eat our dinner at a very fine and unusually nice restaurant, the Quoi D'Ouchy, which was a short walk from our hotel. Maybe it was because we were hungry, but the food seemed exceptional. Luke had a cheese omelet that actually melted in her mouth. I know because along with my delectable veal picatto, I snitched half of her omelet. Chris and Robin stayed at the hotel and fared well in the food department.

When we returned from our dinner and a long walk, it was perhaps midnight. Robin was full of vim and vigor. She wanted to have the sun turned on so she could go out into the park near the hotel and play. Enough of this horsing around for her, and after a physically disciplinary measure, a good whack on her backside, she was finally persuaded to grab her blanket and hit the sack.

Our principal purpose for stopping in Lausanne was to check on the older girls' schools and accommodations so that when we returned from our cruise in the Adriatic, all would be in readiness. We commenced the checkout procedure early the next day by visiting the Chateau de Vennes and meeting Madame Junod. I'm sure she was absolutely overwhelmed when the whole clan arrived on her doorstep. However, being a woman of refinement and regal manner, she greeted us with warmth and enthusiasm and did remarkably well hiding her amazement at the size of the Burns clan.

After seeing the chateau and conversing in French with this truly charming lady, we were thoroughly convinced and pleased that our young ladies would be in excellent hands until they were dispersed to their respective schools.

That evening found us searching for a typical small Swiss restaurant that served the specialties of the country. Our efforts were rewarded when after many inquiries, about both where and how to find it, we ended up in a subcellar of the Hotel Palmiers in a Carnoztel. The room was attractively decorated in the old Swiss rough-hewn log motif with wooden tables and benches along with a huge open fireplace to counteract the dampness of the cellar. It was a place that the typical tourist would not find.

"Hi, Mr. Burns! How are you and Mrs. Burns?" was the enthusiastic reception we received. As our eyes became accustomed to the dimness of the place, I really was dumbfounded and couldn't believe my ears or eyes when I looked at the attractive young girl who approached us from across the room. I recognized Prudence Adams, the niece of our most intimate friends and neighbors, Bob and Nickie Crecca. We had a real old-fashioned get-together and in a matter of minutes found out all about her travels with a student group. We didn't want to monopolize Prudy or take her away from her very attractive friends, so we bid her bon voyage and slipped over to a corner to enjoy our raclette and beef fondue.

Our meal was delicious, and we drank some excellent local Swiss wine. After squaring away *l'addition*, which by the way was very reasonable, we decided we should walk back to the hotel to get rid of some of the calories we had hoarded during dinner. Fortunately, it was downhill, and the two or three miles back to the Montana was negotiated without any mental or physical breakdowns.

The next day our car caravan was scheduled to go to Gstaad to check in with Madame Bouchaud, directress of Institut Montesano. The caravan idea was shot down when Robin fell and broke one of her top front teeth. Luckily, Luke had the name of an American-trained dentist, Dr. Fitting, and he agreed by telephone to look at Robin to make sure there was no serious injury. Once again, the gods smiled on our wandering clan, and after a series of X-rays, careful prodding, and close examination, Dr. Fitting pronounced Robin fit to continue her travels. He was thorough and very capable, yet his bill was quite modest.

While Robin was being examined by the dentist, I took Julie, Laurie, and Tom with me in the Volkswagen Squareback sedan up the mountains to Gstaad. We were favored by a gloriously warm and sunny day. The mountains were deep green interspersed with vivid patches of brightly colored wildflowers. We were seeing truly picture-postcard scenery.

The deterrent to these idyllic surroundings was the erratic drivers who crowded the narrow, winding roads. I classify them in two categories: those who hog the road to prevent anyone else from passing, and those who are going to pass anything and everything regardless of time or place. These fearless Fangios particularly love to honk and pass on the inside of a curve.

However, fortune smiled on us and we arrived safely with time to spare before meeting with Madame Bouchard, which gave us time to drive all through the little town. I think Laurie and Julie were very happy with what they saw. I pointed out some of the various ski areas and could see the gleam in their eyes as they imagined themselves hurtling down these slopes during the coming winter. For that matter, I, too, could picture myself bouncing from mogul to mogul on a crisp, wintry morning. Back to reality, we drove up the very narrow, unpaved road to the main chalet at Montesano.

Madame arrived as we did. Our business at Montesano was quickly transacted. Laurie got a quick look at the chalet she was going to live in, and back we loaded into the car for our return to Lausanne.

We took a different road on our way back so we could drive through the Col du Pillon to view the huge glacier that nestles between rocky peaks. Our lunch on the way back in a roadside chalet was miserable and expensive, served without grace or any of the supposedly famous Swiss hospitality. I wish I could remember the name of that joint so I could warn fellow travelers from a potentially sad experience.

After our return from Gstaad, we had only one more duty to perform. Wendi had to be taken to the Chateau Brillantmont to familiarize herself with her school and meet Mademoiselle Fourney. The visit to Brillantmont was a pleasant surprise. We liked Mlle. Fourney immensely and were extremely impressed with the facilities. For that matter, we finally concluded that although all the girls had done exceedingly well with their schools, Wendi had done the best. The visit served to allay the fears and trepidation that she had had before.

The rest of our time in Lausanne was spent walking through all parts of the city, morning, afternoon, and evening. The most interesting section was near the university. There I gained an unfortunate impression of the young student and traveler. To me the ugly male tourist looks feminine and sloppy. He has long, shoulder-length hair, unpressed clothes, and an unwashed look. The female has long, shoulder-length hair, unpressed clothes, and an unwashed look. The only difference is that the male's beard is longer. Frankly, these so-called ambassadors of goodwill and neighborliness are so screwed up with their own self-importance that they care little about the impression they leave on others.

A word of advice to fellow travelers: don't change your money at your hotel. Those canny, crafty Swiss innkeepers will give you about 2 to 3 percent less than the bank will. In one case, when we were checking out early in the morning, we received 4.12 francs to the dollar instead of the official rate of 4.30 available at the bank. That's eighteen francs or about four dollars that we were "taken" for. It's worse in Italy, as I was yet to learn.

We weren't sad about leaving Lausanne because we knew we'd return in six weeks. Our departure was by train and, other than a mad scramble to get our reserved space in the first-class section where we had to rout out trespassers, everything clicked with usual Swiss precision.

The view from the train going along the Rhone River valley and the Italian Alps—after passing through the Simplon tunnel—is absolutely breathtaking.

The whole trip to Milan, although long in hours, went rapidly because of the magnificent vistas that appeared at every curve.

Our wait in the Milan railroad station was as unique an experience as I've ever had. We had an hour to waste, and I spent it playing my favorite game, People Watching.

The most significant fact I learned while playing was that Italian railroad cars have an absolutely unlimited capacity. When they're full to the limit with people, bags, boxes, and whatnot, along will come three more people. After much gesticulating with arms and hands, never seen before by this ordinary American, the carriage door will open and the three or four people are swallowed inside, along with the bags, boxes, and whatnots. The Italian railroad cars just seem to digest people.

I found out more about this congestion when I walked from our car to claim our reserved space in the dining car. We had to go through six carriages of human mass to reach our destination. In doing so it is necessary to give what you get, and that is many, many helpful pushes directed at one's rear region. In America we call it goosing. In Italy it's called being helpful. If you get into the swing of things and join in the fun, you'll be amazed at the interesting people you will get to know on an intimate basis.

Eating on an Italian train is an experience everyone should have at one time or another. My first time was enough to last me a lifetime. I won't say the food is thrown at you, but it comes fast and, fortunately, with great accuracy. Our waiter played outfield for the Milan Mets and was great at the plate. The food is fried in grease that saw its sweet day in the time of Caesar. I must admit that the spaghetti was good, but the veal, chicken, and the rest just shouldn't have happened. When the bill arrived, I was shocked at the price, but I paid and decided the walk to the diner and back, playing backside patty-cake, was worth the overcharge.

By the time we arrived in Venice, we had organized ourselves à la Italian for the contest of baggage hurling. This is done by one member of the team rushing outside the carriage, grabbing a porter, and then planting the porter and himself under the compartment window. Then the members of the team inside throw the baggage out the window and hope their teammates on the ground are good receivers. I was very proud of our team. We did right well, and although we weren't the first to unload, we came in a close second.

In Venice we piled our crew into a speedboat. I use the term loosely, but they are faster than the gondolas. We were deposited on the doorstep of the Luna Hotel. Here we had reservations, but with usual Italian efficiency they were fouled up. By this time I had learned that if you move your arms and hands rapidly with imagination, you can solve any problem. Not only did my fantastic movements get us our rooms, but one of the motions I made, and I'm sorry to say I forget which one, earned us a discount on our room charge. It must have been a pip, because I knocked ten thousand lire per day off the originally quoted rate.

Once again we were elated at the sanctuary our hotel provided and especially the chance to clean the train and travel grime from our now toughened hides. We were particularly pleased with the Luna Hotel in that once the mix-up of the reservations was behind us, everything else went very smoothly.

We ate a well-served, delicious meal in the hotel dining room and then decided to walk off the calories. Walking in Venice has its fascinations as well as problems. The causes of both are the same, narrow twisting meandering pathways called streets.

This first night we lucked out in that I had bought a map of the city and by concentrated use of its information, were able to wander about quite freely.

Upon our return to the Luna, we received a telephone call from Ed and Mary Crane, people from Newport Beach who had just arrived in Venice on board the boat we were to charter, the *Cuhona*. They had been out to dinner in Venice and volunteered to drop by our hotel that same evening. Since they were leaving early the next morning, we gratefully accepted their offer to meet us and introduce us to the captain of the *Cuhona*.

They arrived, and Mary deftly took Luke aside to give her the lowdown on everyone and everything while I went to the bar with Ed, Bill Langley, their two boys, and the captain.

Actually, we were very pleased with the captain, Cornelius Marys, and he appeared to have the makings of a fine companion as well as being a capable and well-trained charter boat skipper. There was one problem, however. The Cranes told us the cook was absolutely beyond salvage. The only reason he hadn't been beached before was that no one knew where he had hidden all the galley utensils. Even the skipper wouldn't defend him.

We exchanged other tidbits of information with the Cranes and then bid each other bon voyage, they to return to the United States, and we to board the *Cuhona*.

Luke and I wrestled with the problem of the cook that evening and decided to sleep on it before coming to any conclusion. When morning arrived and before we were even out of bed, we looked at each other and simultaneously said, "Let's fire the cook!"

Armed with determination, we corralled the troops, and after bargaining with the captain of a "speedboat" that we hired by the hour, we churned along the waters of the Grand Canal, out into one of the many mail channels on our way to the Quai St. Elena to find the *Cuhona*.

Captain Marys welcomed us aboard, and while the rest of the crew happily explored our home-to-be, we told the skipper of our decision about the cook. I must say that our request was quickly acted upon, and thus the *Cuhona* suddenly acquired a new master chef and a world-renowned omelet chef and rotisseur, namely Luke and Don Burns.

Now that we had the titles suited to our extraordinary culinary talents, we found that results were going to speak louder than words. The captain was rather noncommittal about suggestions as to quantities as well as varieties, but he did give us the name of a ship's provisioner, a Signor Ligabue.

We left most of our gang aboard the *Cuhona* to help clean ship, and the master chef, her chief assistant, and Chris and Robin piled back into our "speedboat" to tangle with Signor Ligabue and his nest of pirates.

Actually, the personnel at Ligabue's was most helpful. They recommended quantities and variety, and gave our master chef some useful hints about how to prepare some of the pasta dishes in which neither of us specialized. We spent almost two hours provisioning for twelve people for thirty-five days. Frankly, I was bewildered. I didn't know whether we had too much or too little. We were going on a by-guess-and-by-hope basis that we would be able to get some supplies en route, such as veal, milk, fresh vegetables, and fresh fruit. However, we did lay in an ample supply of canned goods as a backup stock.

We left Ligabue's knowing we had accomplished a lot, but just what we'd done besides spend a whole pot of dough, we weren't sure. Our "speedboat" crew, the skipper of which spoke excellent English with an American accent, had by this time truly wormed his way into our affections by babysitting Robin and being extremely gentlemanly to Chris. He didn't try to pinch her and even asked if he might show her the sights of Venice, without charge, by moonlight.

After leaving Ligabue's we were sold a bill of goods on visiting some of the outer islands that surround Venice to see many sights of fascinating interest. Needless to say, we swallowed the bait, collected our gang from the *Cuhona*, and then headed across the calm open waters of the lagoon.

Our first stop was at the island of Burano, where we saw a large church tower that outleaned Pisa's by a good ten degrees. It was here, practically in the path of the falling tower of Burano, where we had a delicious authentic Italian fish lunch. We ate rice soup with cheese and a fish-flavored sauce. Then we were served octopus, eel, sole, scampi, and some other mysteriously flavored morsel that I am sure was squid. We were also served a variety of wonderful white local wines. Truly it was our most delicious repast so far on our trip. The cost was reasonable in that for nine of us and the two members of our speedboat crew, the bill was 13,000 lire—or just under $20.

On our way back to our private speedboat, we stopped by a school run by a church where small girls starting at the age of seven were instructed on how to sew fancy and commercially saleable tourist-attracting embroidery. All the young girls sat in a room, perhaps twenty by forty feet, with a nun seated at one end in a rather commanding position. She was obviously the head wrangler and whip cracker. Along each wall sat some older women looking like department foremen, and in front of each of these older women sat the young girls, oldest ones in the rear and youngest at the front. They never spoke except to recite in unison different prayers on about a regular half-hour schedule. I slipped a few thousand lire into the kitty and asked the nun to put in a good word for me because I was sure she had better connections with the right people than I had.

We left Burano with a rather saintly spirit and putted through swampland where I was told there was excellent duck hunting in the late fall. I marked this bit of information for further reference and further research.

We then stopped at the island of Torcello, which houses some ancient Greek ruins. We didn't stay long on Torcello because we figured we were going to see the place from whence it had come in the week following.

From Torcello we went to Murano, the island that houses the world-famous glass factories. Our first stop on Murano was in a typical tourist trap. We were met at the boat by a slickly dressed gentleman who ushered us into a chamber that contained a large group of tourists and a small furnace. The glassblower, or master, as he is called, was producing some rather run-of-the-mill, ordinary pieces. After this exhibition we were ushered into the display room, where it was clearly and rather crudely indicated that we were expected to buy something. Perhaps a little more pressure was put on our group because we came in a private launch rather than on one of the cattle boats. Fortunately, we resisted the high pressures of their sales department and had the speedboat take us to the factory that had been recommended by the Bents.

We arrived at the Salviati & Company factory, and after being escorted through a very clean, modern little facility, had the wonderful experience of watching a real master at work. He, with four assistants and two apprentices, was in the process of creating a life-size glass mallard. It was exquisite, and I purchased it before it was even finished.

The master put my name on it and signed the piece with his own, Savon.

It had been a long and fruitful day, but the Luna Hotel looked especially good on our return. I was wrung out, but a cold shower and a truly fine dinner in the hotel dining room gave us all enough energy for our usual evening stroll and so to bed.

The following day we decided to try to get to know Venice and sallied forth from the hotel with much vigor but no map. After two hours of strolling through winding and torturously twisting streets we were hopelessly lost. We couldn't even find a place to buy a map, and every time we asked one of our Venetian hosts where we were, we got a blank stare along with a "No spika da Engleesh." I was really worried when we turned out of one narrow alley onto a broad boulevard and nearly got run over by a car. Then I knew we were in trouble.

Finally, we came upon a railroad track, and after flipping a coin to determine which direction to take, we walked the ties, hoping it would lead us to the main station from which we could catch a launch back to the Luna Hotel. We lucked out. Our haggard band finally and with a huge sigh of relief stumbled into a boat, sprawled out in the closest corner, and was whisked effortlessly back to our hotel. Brute force was necessary to move them from the boat to a restaurant near the Luna, but with the help of Pete Niggeman, who had just joined us, we kept everyone moving.

That afternoon Luke and I went on another exploratory venture, but this time we took a map. With the aid of this vital navigation device we went to visit two more showrooms of the Murano glass factories. The first had nothing unusual. In the second I found a beautiful, white glass, flying seagull that I couldn't resist. On the excuse that it would be for my new office, I purchased the piece and had it sent directly home. That purchase was a wonderful climax to our Venetian venture, and all that was left to do was go back to the hotel and wait for the next day, our getaway day aboard the *Cuhona*.

CHAPTER SIX

Wednesday, August 3, 1966

Dawn came with a bright flash of golden sun thrust across the rippled blue waters of the Grand Canal. This was the day. It was no problem to rouse the clan. They were raring to go. Pete and Tom were up and on their way to the boat by seven o'clock. I paid the hotel bill and was badly taken on the exchange, but I was too full of good cheer to argue. Those Italians are just going to take you one way or the other. I figured I might as well smile and enjoy the inevitable. I smiled, but secretly I didn't enjoy it one bit.

Our arrival aboard the *Cuhona* was a masterpiece of confusion. Bags were thrown aboard. There was a scramble for bunks. Everyone changed from city duds to seagoing bikinis. We were aboard our home for the next thirty-five days and damnably glad of it.

We stowed all our gear and familiarized ourselves with all the various intricacies of the yacht. The captain left to get our clearance from Italy, and we filled the water tank. While most of the crew kept busy, I started to fret about the whereabouts of our load of supplies. Just as I was about to get into a real stew, around the bend in the canal came a heavily loaded barge that headed directly for the *Cuhona*. At first I thought it might be for us, but then I was sure that they could have brought the relatively small amount that we'd ordered in a standard launch. I was wrong. Seated on top of a mound of boxes was a smiling and waving Mr. Ligabue. Along with our provisioner was a smartly dressed and very watchful policeman to guard our goods.

Mr. Ligabue jauntily hopped off the barge, and before I could ask any questions, the barge's crew was wildly throwing cartons, crates, cans, and sacks on board with the usual Italian abandon. These guys would have been great on a train. The stuff just kept coming and coming. Mr.

Ligabue's smile became broader and wider while I began to sink lower and lower into despair as I could see my pocketbook shrinking into nonexistence. I think we got what we ordered, but Luke to this day is convinced they doubled all that we requested as they double a bill when dealing with rich Americans. Mr. Ligabue was not at all sympathetic to our two-and-a-half-nickel problem as he presented me with the bill. Long ago I had decided to be philosophical about this money problem, and it was well that I was or I would have sent the barge-load back, packed up our gear, gone to the train or plane, and called the whole thing off. Naturally, none of this was possible, so we left Mr. Ligabue. He was wealthier, wiser, and self-satisfied. We were poorer, wiser, and rarin' to go.

The captain returned while the mountains of provisions were still on deck, and at first glance he threw up his hands and indicated we'd never get it all stowed. After a few calming and reassuring words, we all pitched in and with great effort stowed everything in all the nooks and crannies throughout the *Cuhona*.

With the hard work behind us, and wads of money liberally sprinkled from Switzerland to Venice, we hauled up the anchor and with a jaunty toot of the ship's horn, were under way.

Our trip to Trieste was beautiful. The sun was bright, the sea was calm, and there was just enough breeze to beat the heat. We traveled past beautiful beaches loaded with Italian bathers. It took about five and a half hours to make the voyage from Venice to Trieste, and every minute of this leg was thoroughly enjoyed by all.

As we approached Trieste, we detoured slightly to the north so we could pass right under the cliff on which was perched Maximilian's beautiful and well-preserved palace. From there we skirted the shoreline, and after passing through a relatively inactive harbor, unusual because of its size, we berthed near the naval base, away from the sewer outlets in a fairly quiet spot.

The only thing that marred our solitude was a mechanic racing one of the Italian navy patrol-boat engines.

That evening we had our first meal on board prepared by the master chef and her ingenious assistant. Since the lamb that Mr. Ligabue had sold us by the carcass wouldn't fit in the freezer or refrigerator, we had it roasted and liberally seasoned with wine, brandy, bitters, and beer. If I am permitted a modest comment, I must say it was delicious. At least everyone pushed themselves away from the tables we had set on the afterdeck with a look of satiated satisfaction. We had eaten so much that we had to force ourselves to walk through the city.

We climbed to a large castle surrounded by a fortress wall that enclosed an old city and a square of ancient Roman ruins. All the areas were brightly lit with modern, effective lighting to heighten our viewing pleasure. By the time we got back to the *Cuhona*, we were tired and ready for bed. Even my hard rocklike mattress that I was soon to know and appreciate intimately was welcome, and it didn't deter me from falling sound asleep immediately.

Thursday, August 4, 1966

We raised ourselves early the next morning because we had to go to the local open-air market to buy the day's needed fresh supplies. The captain joined us, and with his good Italian, my imaginative hand waving, and Luke's practiced buyer's eye, we had little if any trouble getting what we wanted. We purchased the bread, which was not for sale in the open-air market, at a shop that was very difficult to find. However, it was worth it because it was superb, especially the dark wheat loaves. On our way back to the *Cuhona* we bought a washboard to do our own laundry and some film for all cameras—particularly Polaroid—and cleared our papers with the harbormaster. It was very easy, so without further complications we set sail for Yugoslavia.

After an hour's cruise from Trieste we arrived at the small port of Koper. Here we were greeted by a friendly, cheerful harbormaster and an equally affable policeman. They were invited on board, and with sign language, a few words of broken Italian, a few cigarettes, and two uncirculated Kennedy half-dollars, we became fast friends. Two more dour-looking, officious-acting men arrived. A man in plain clothes was from the secret police, and a man in uniform was an immigrations agent. Because they did not exude the spirit of welcome that their compatriots had, we didn't extend ourselves beyond a social drink of beer. I think they would have camped on board all day if we had let them, but since we had shoved our passports and crew and passenger list under their noses, they got the idea that we'd like to move on. All four men left the ship with all our passports. I had moments of apprehension, but the skipper told us not to concern ourselves, that they would be back—and they were, two and a half hours later. They probably went home for lunch first. Again all four officials boarded us, sat down at the table on the afterdeck, and were served a beer. They finally handed us our passports and we indicated we wanted to move on. With a handshake from our two friends and a salute from the other two, they left, and we quickly hauled in our docking lines and headed out of the harbor to Piran.

Again, the weather was perfect. Our voyage from Koper to Piran was smooth, sunny, and enjoyable. We passed close by some fancy hotel resorts that were packed with people lying on the rocky beaches worshipping the sun. We arrived at Piran in the early evening and entered the harbor through a breakwater that looked so narrow that I was afraid it would not accommodate our vessel. I was wrong as usual, and we charged through and then coasted up to a long quay. In no time with the boys assisting, the skipper and Tim, our steward-galley cleaner-pot walloper, had us secured fast to the wharf.

I found out how the animals in a zoo feel. No sooner were we secure than hundreds of vacationers started to file by the boat, peeking into windows and ports. After this experience I think the animals probably have more fun looking at people than people do watching them. This was People Watching at its best. Most of them looked with open-mouthed, awed expressions. Some were sullen and appeared to harbor jealous resentment. However, most were idly curious and appeared pleasant and friendly. We noticed that a great deal of German was spoken and that most of the cars on the streets had German registrations. Undoubtedly, Piran was in the process of being discovered by the rest of Europe. I had to agree it was a charming and fascinating small seaside community.

Our master chef and her assistant outdid themselves by preparing roast chicken à la *Cuhona*. That's chicken roasted by guess and by golly with every seasoning on board, plus liberal bastings with wine, brandy, butter, bitters, and beer.

Our walk that evening was short and sweet. The town is very small, and all the activity was centered along a promenade on the beachfront. There was a rock-and-roll group at one of the hotels playing the latest American songs and singing the words in English. It was funny to hear because the beat was slightly off and the words just didn't come out the way we would expect. They interspersed their interpretations of our latest export with wild and woolly polkas and local dances. At midnight, like Cinderella's coach, everyone disappeared and we returned to the *Cuhona* for our needed sleep.

Friday, August 5, 1966

Again we were blessed with a perfect day for cruising and the skipper promised us some very interesting sights on our way to Pula from Piran. We threaded through small groups of islands, and at a signal from the skipper there would be a mad dash for binoculars. I, of course, pulled rank. We'd pass close by a colony of sun worshippers who wore topless and bottomless bikinis. The consensus among all the crew was that with a rare few exceptions it would have been much better from a viewer's standpoint if these nudists had at least worn bikinis. When there is nothing left to the imagination, there's almost nothing.

One interesting aspect was that a great number of these sun lovers were tanned all over except for a badly sunburned area on their bosoms and their middles. Too much of that and the fun certainly would go out of their holidays.

Just before pulling into Pula we passed an island that was Marshal Tito's summer residence. The island was surrounded by six heavily armed, fast patrol boats that kept all intended interlopers at least three miles away.

Pula has one extremely ancient relic to attract the curious: a well-preserved coliseum. That Roman amphitheater is supposed to be in better condition than the one in Rome.

We docked within 150 yards of this edifice of the past, and as soon as lines were secured and proper attire was put on, we trooped as a group to view the ruins. The closer we came, the more history permeated the air. For a price of 625 dinar (50¢ U.S.) we were all admitted. We climbed some well-worn and well-traveled stairs that were probably trod by early Christians on their way to destruction on the floor of the arena. As we reached the historic pit of death and struggle, our illusions were shattered. The whole arena floor was covered with folding chairs in preparation for a rock concert or, as it was billed, a "battle of the bands." The historic effect was ruined and we left, disappointed that we couldn't commune more realistically with the past.

That evening the assistant chef, rotisseur extraordinaire, concocted a delicious dish of minced lamb. We had to get rid of the remaining lamb Mr. Ligabue had dumped on us, so I cut it into strips about two inches long. It was then browned in olive oil. I prepared a sauce of brandy, orange liqueur, Angostura bitters, various herbs and spices, a bottle of Chianti, and one bottle of Italy's best white wine. We let the whole concoction stew for about two hours.

With it, the chef prepared a fresh lettuce-and-tomato salad. Between the two dishes and some excellent hearth-baked white bread, we once again enjoyed high praise from all our crew.

We walked through the town and saw a most interesting ancient Roman arch and a carefully preserved Greek temple. Both were magnificent. On our return to the *Cuhona* we found that quite a crowd had collected around the boat and that Julie was conversing in French with a Yugoslav who was asking all kinds of questions about America. I hadn't been back more than five minutes when I was approached by two neatly attired, clean-cut gentlemen. They asked me a great many questions about the boat, admired her lines and construction, and were interested in many of its engineering aspects. They were obviously highly trained men and spoke English, French, and German.

I really broke the ice when I took their picture with a colored Polaroid camera. Because it was at night and I used a flash, the picture did not turn out at all well. Even so they were amazed and hesitantly asked for it as a souvenir. I gladly gave it to them and signed it with my name and address.

The conversation turned to the war in Vietnam. They asked me my opinion. I said that although none of us liked it, our national honor was at stake and we just had to put up or shut up. They seemed satisfied with the answer and added that they knew someone had to stand against the Chinese. One of the men added that in his opinion the masses of Yugoslavia supported the U.S. stand, at least in their hearts. No one, he further indicated, wanted to express this support vocally.

I then asked them if they would be offended if I gave them a memento of our visit. When they seemed pleased, I gave each of them an uncirculated Kennedy half-dollar. I could not have given them anything better. They were as pleased as kids with an electric train for Christmas. We again exchanged names and addresses, and they sadly bid us good night.

I thought that was the last I was to see of my newfound, delightful friends, but I guessed wrong. They reappeared in about thirty minutes and quickly handed me a beautifully carved small wooden box, shook my hand, and immediately left. I was very touched and pleased with my gift. I wished to thank them again and vowed to write to them when I returned to the United States.

The next day we were to pay for all the delightful weather we had had to date.

Saturday, August 6, 1966

Although the sky was clear, the wind at seven in the morning was blowing at about twenty knots. We quickly concluded our port formalities and passed the shipyards, submarines, and forts that guard Pula, and hit a very heavy sea just outside. The wind picked up to force 5 or 6, and the sea was whipped to a frothy white. Most of the crew were laid out flat on the deck of the salon. Robin stayed on deck with me, and we would laugh uproariously when we'd hit a particularly solid wave or take a precarious roll. We slugged through about thirty miles of open water and finally reached the haven of an island lee. Shortly thereafter we dropped anchor in a lovely little cove, launched the Zodiac rubber boat, and all dove in for swimming and skin diving. We lay in the quiet of this cove for four hours before dashing out into the storm again. We had a three-hour run to Rab, our port for the night. Luckily the wind had moderated so that although we had anticipated another rough passage, it turned out to be only mildly choppy. Robin didn't get one real belly laugh because of the lack of any wild motion of the boat.

The approaches to Rab are very impressive. The city is old and dominated by a high wall from the sea side that is topped with an ancient fort. The harbor is snug and well protected from all sides. We moored along the quay, using the spot normally occupied by a hydrofoil. This dock had two ramps for loading and unloading. The ramps were rail high to our boat.

Shortly after we were secured, people started to promenade up one ramp, look us over, and then serenely walk out the other without any comment whatsoever. I wanted to sell tickets, but Luke dissuaded me, saying I'd probably end up in the jug for selling tickets without permission from the local commissar.

All during dinner, which consisted of a masterfully prepared roast beef, canned vegetable salad, and fresh fruit for dessert, we had people trooping up one ramp and down the other. Once in a while a good-looking gal would go by and the looked-at would appreciate a good-looker.

Tiring of the caged feeling that descended upon us from being on public display, we decided to join the masses. We left the ship and wandered down toward the center of activity, which as usual was a rock-and-roll band mixing in a few local favorites with the standard imports "Paperback Writer" and "Motorcycle Bounce." These people didn't have the antics of the watusi or the "surfers' shuffle" yet, but I figured that particular U.S. export would be along shortly. Again, at the magic hour of midnight everyone disappeared as we did by drifting back to the boat.

Sunday, August 7, 1966

The weather once again favored us, and we left this beautiful little city surrounded by its fortress walls and green hills to immediately emerge into some of the most desolate, bare, rocky coast that I've ever seen. It looked like the recent Surveyor pictures of the moon. There was absolutely no visible life or vegetation for a distance of thirty miles. Because the scenery offered no interest to keep the crew occupied, we towed the kids on the rubber rafts behind the *Cuhona*. It was great fun, especially when they surfed down the breaking waves of the ship's wake. When the excitement of wake surfing died down, we broke out the water skis. By the time we all had a try at water skiing, some more successfully than others, we had covered almost thirty miles and it was time for lunch. We pulled alongside one of the bare, rocky islands to swim and eat. After lunch we were again under way, heading for Zadar.

Arrival in Zadar was very ordinary. The city from the sea looked modern and dowdy. On closer inspection the bomb damage that occurred during World War II was apparent everywhere.

We moored next to a quay that bordered the wall surrounding the old portion of the city. That wall was marred along its entire surface with bullet, mortar, and small anti-tank shells.

We sat on the afterdeck exchanging stares with the populace. The most noticeable impression that we all gained from this mini-metropolis was the profusion of rather sloppily dressed soldiers. They wore unkempt baggy green uniforms and wrinkled, sweat-stained garrison hats. At least they had haircuts of decent length. Interspersed among the slovenly green groups were a few very nattily dressed men wearing smartly pressed air force blue uniforms.

The assistant chef was delegated that evening to prepare from scratch a sauce for the spaghetti. Since there was no ground meat available, I cut up one of the roast beefs and put it through a hand grinder. I then lightly browned the ground beef. To this I added four cans of skinned tomatoes and six finely chopped onions. I crushed three garlic cloves and threw those in. Three dashes of Crosse & Blackwell sauce was followed by two beef bouillon cubes. Liberal sprinklings of oregano, rosemary, thyme, and a few other miscellaneous flavors preceded the addition of half a bottle of red wine, Angostura bitters, half a glass of cherry brandy, one-fourth bottle of beer, and half a glass of Bristol cream sherry. This mixture, which would rival Al Capp's Kickapoo Joy Juice, was left simmering in a very hot oven for four hours. Modesty forbids me to say how fantastically well this culinary creation was received. I will say that everyone gorged to the gills before being hoisted from the table for their evening walk.

We strolled into the old part of town and for the first time didn't hear the lilting strains of any rock-and-roll. Perhaps the fact that it was Sunday night had something to do with this serenity.

In the heart of Zadar we saw a truly old but newly excavated Greek city. Mixed in with these Grecian ruins were more up-to-date Roman remains. Within proximity of the Roman buildings was an old Byzantine church and a more modern, three-hundred-year-old Catholic church. This whole area, which covered perhaps twenty acres, was enclosed with modern, post-World War II apartment buildings. In an area of less than half a square mile paraded history from before Christ to the present day.

Monday, August 8, 1966

Even though Zadar was an architect's paradise, the drabness of the populace dominated by the badly clad, green-uniformed soldiers made us eager to get under way. After filling the tanks with water and taking a taxi to buy ice, we hauled aboard our lines and happily left Zadar.

We had a six-hour ride to the spectacular fresh waterfalls two miles up the River Krka from the inland city of Skradin. We reached Skradin by cruising through the narrow entrance of the harbor at Sibenik and then along a series of inland lagoons connected by deep, rock-lined gorges. The scenery was heroic in the sense that it was a small saltwater version of the Grand Canyon. We proceeded about twelve miles up these series of ravines from salt to fresh water. We anchored about a half mile below the lower series of falls. These waterfalls tumble down in a series of steps for five hundred feet over a distance of almost a mile. They are truly magnificent.

We all piled from the *Cuhona*, some swimming against the current, others aboard the Zodiac, and proceeded to the base of the falls.

I hopped from the Zodiac and secured it to a small bush next to the river. I then waded into deeper water to swim, leaving Luke behind. I turned around at the sound of a piercing whistle to see a man on the bridge that crosses the river below the falls. He would point to Luke, then himself, and then mime a frantic breaststroke. Luke got the idea and hurried over to Peter for protection. We all decided that although this lakeside lothario had ideas of breaststroking, perhaps they weren't connected with swimming and water but with woods and a hidden glen.

Having discouraged Yugoslavia's greatest lover, and having had Luke's ego inflated to the bursting point, we swam to the falls to luxuriate in the cool, clear, fresh-falling torrents. There were thousands of people enjoying this natural playground, yet the grandeur of this wonderland was completely unspoiled. We stayed until the last possible minute, swimming and gliding down the river with the current time and again.

We upped anchor in time to make our next destination, a small, landlocked cove five miles south of the small city of Rogoynicce before darkness set in.

We let one of the apprentice chefs, Pete, help the master chef prepare beef Stroganoff for dinner. Since I was banned from the galley during the preparation of this dish, I am not able to divulge its contents. I must, with all professional honesty, admit that it was delectable. I had two helpings just to make the apprentice chef feel there was a future for him in the galley. Because we anchored out in this cove, we were unable to take our usual evening walk. We substituted an after-dinner swim and found the water delightfully warm, phosphorescent, and invigorating.

Tuesday, August 9, 1966

To earn breakfast the next morning, everyone had to jump overboard for a quick, fast-awakening dip. We had a few laggards on board, but finally hunger drove them to the depths. After we had all cleaned ourselves, the dishes, and the boat, Luke and I went to the shore for our daily hike.

We walked up into the rocky hills that were cultivated with many small plots of grapevines and small orchards of fig trees. While trying to ascend a particularly steep section of the hill, we cut through a small vineyard and immediately heard a noise like the braying of a donkey. Then we saw two old women approaching us with fists waving. We retreated from their vineyard: they still pursued us. I finally stood my ground, tipped my hat, and smiled. This must have confused them, because their attack fell apart and they made a strategic withdrawal.

We climbed to the top of the hill and saw a most memorable panorama: to the west lay the sea dotted with a hundred or more islands of various sizes; to the south and east lay the *Cuhona* riding peacefully at anchor in the small, fully protected, deepwater cove; to the east and north lay the ruggedly beautiful mountains that would be a guerrilla fighter's heaven.

As we were returning to the *Cuhona*, we saw two old women herding a small flock of sheep. They were carrying some ripe figs. One of them carried a large, full basket and the other had a small sack. Since we were unable to converse with them, we called on the lingual skills of the skipper. He quickly found out that although they did not want money, they would barter their figs for rice. We agreed. The skipper took the figs to the ship and returned with the rice. The woman with the larger basket broke open one of the boxes and took some of its contents so she would receive a greater share. We last saw these women herding their goats among some other fig trees while they replenished their supply.

It was in this small, well-protected, remote cove that we made a major archaeological find. Lonnie, age ten, with faceplate and snorkel, was cruising on the surface and hollered for someone to go down in about twenty feet of water to bring up a suspected piece of an amphora. Everyone but Tim, our steward, was skeptical. He dove down and, by golly, brought up the mouth and neck, with handle attached, of an amphora jar. This find really started an enthusiastic hunt for all objects of antiquity.

Reluctantly, we left our sheltered retreat and steamed full bore to Split. There was a force 4 or 5 wind on our tail, which helped us cover the twenty-off miles in excellent time. On arrival at this large and seemingly modern city, we passed a British cruise ship, the *Andes*. Fortunately, it was in the process of leaving and the city was partially emptied of tourists.

After mooring the stern to the quay in front of a modern, Hilton-type hotel, we all went ashore to walk through the town. Our first venture took us toward the yacht club, where there was a surprising number of small sailboats, about fifteen feet in length. These boats had a blunted bow, were all painted blue, and were fitted with badly shaped cotton sails. The crews of the little class boats were early teenagers who were just having a ball. They typified the young sailing fanatics I've seen all over the United States.

We tried to walk past the little shipyard adjacent to the yacht club, but were stopped by an old man who I thought was selling lottery tickets. I found out what a real barrier language can be: by the time I figured out he was selling ten-cent admission tickets to a special beach, he was shouting at me and I was sore at him. In English he didn't understand, I told him just where he could place each and every one of his little pink tickets. After leaving the man and his book of g.d. tickets, we were about to make a wrong turn again but stopped just as a guard, wearing an automatic small-caliber rifle slung menacingly over his shoulder, took a few bold steps toward us. Obviously this soldier had the authority and the means of enforcement to carry out whatever he wanted our group to do. Besides, he might understand English, and that could create a first-class international incident. I behaved myself and at a considerable loss of prestige among my crew, decided discretion was better than a fat lip. We retreated without challenging this man of authority.

Half the troops decided they would eat ashore on the assumption that too much of our deliciously prepared food was not good for the waistline. Those who ate on board had excellent steaks that had been marinated in honey and brandy.

That night after walking through the ancient part of Split, we decided that the city was aptly named. It is a schizophrenic city with a completely split personality. One side was old and represented by the beautiful ruins of Diocletian's palace, the old Roman sulfur baths, and the antiquated but still used marketplace. The other side was reflected in modern—to an extreme—apartment buildings, hotels, and a futuristic lighthouse that dominated the south side of the harbor. There was no meshing of these two extremes. It was either very old or post-war modern and futuristic.

Wednesday, August 10, 1966

We arose early the next morning to beat the crowd at the marketplace, where we had to buy bread, fresh vegetables, wine, and other daily necessities. Although we were there a few minutes after six, the whole area was crowded with vendors, lookers, and buyers. It is quite an experience to shop in one of these markets. Half the time we were really taken because of language difficulties, and the other half of the time people had some compassion and overcharged only us moderately. When prices were marked on the merchandise, I did real well—I paid full price. Of course, the locals used these marked prices as a point from which to bargain. We did the best buying to date in Split and came away from the market very pleased with our Yankee trading abilities.

While the skipper cleared us for departure and went visiting with an old friend, we went back to Diocletian's palace for a closer look at its vastness and architectural splendor. For 200 dinars each we were admitted to the huge underground vaults, storage rooms, and wine cellars. Only part of the original structure had been excavated, but that which we viewed impressed us no end even though most of it was damp, dark, and covered with slime of the ages.

On our way back to the *Cuhona* we stopped in a local restaurant for some refreshments. We found that great patience was needed to patronize any of the local pubs, because it took a lackadaisical young lady forty-two minutes to bring us two beers, three Pepsis, two lemonades, and one coffee. If it had not been for Pete's persistent prodding and frequent trips to remind this mismanaged maiden that we would like what we ordered, I think we would have waited an hour.

Just before getting under way for Hvar we went on a wine-buying trip back near the marketplace. While waiting in line, which necessitated constant jockeying to maintain anywhere near your turn, the fumes and fragrance of the wines gave us a cheap drunk. The air in these very small, confined shops must be at least fifty proof. I didn't know what to order, so I ordered what the man ahead of me ordered when he had a ten-liter jug filled. After two of our own bottles had been filled with the same stuff, Tim asked if it was a table wine. Somehow we found that it was a brandy of some sort and fortunately had our other four bottles filled with a white, young, but better-than-average local wine.

Upon returning to the *Cuhona* we tried some of the brandy. Wow! Those bottles contained Yugoslavian white lightning. Even the skipper, a man of strong physical capacity, was shaken to his very roots as the brandy burned its way to the hollowness of his gut. I tasted it and shuddered for several minutes before coming up for air.

On our way to Hvar we ran into some moderately choppy seas. Because we didn't feel any compulsion to get anywhere at any particular time, we turned our stern to the sea and in an hour's time pulled out of the main channel and ducked behind a small island. There we found a delightfully calm refuge surrounded on all sides by vine-covered hills. The shoreline dropped precipitously into the bay, allowing us to anchor with a line running to a large boulder on the beach. Once secure, we all dove overboard into the delightfully warm but refreshing water of a hidden lagoon. By this time, Robin, clad in her bright orange life jacket, always joined our swimming parties—for that matter she wanted to be first in and last out.

Because some of the gang had missed my epicurean masterpiece of the previous evening, by popular demand I was prevailed upon to give a repeat performance. By this time the diners were becoming more critical because of the excellent training their palates had received during the previous gastronomic delights. I went all out. Every regular seasoning, aperitif, and before-, during-, and after-dinner alcoholic beverages were included in the marinade, along with honey, mustard, curry, and even Bovril beef stock concentrate. It was absolutely my crowning achievement. Pete ate three steaks and the captain and Tim two each. In the course of their meal those three polished off three bottles of Italian red wine.

Thursday, August 11, 1966

Swimming was the first order of business, followed by our usual continental-type breakfast. Pete found the top and handle of an amphora jug. The proportions of these graceful containers, at least as represented by the parts we gathered, always pleased my unartistic eye. We left for Hvar after thoroughly examining the floor of this inlet. Unfortunately, we didn't discover any more archaeological wonders, but we did find an empty lobster trap.

Hvar, on first impression, seemed like many of the other old walled towns we had visited. The main difference here was the location where we moored. It was the choice spot so far on our trip in that all the people going to and from the beach had to pass immediately astern of our grandstand seats. By this time we had perfected our People Watching to the point where we were grading the female pulchritude on a scale of one to ten. Ten was an impossible score to give, and a seven would give Marilyn Monroe a run for her calendar. At one point we did get very magnanimous and give out one or two sevens.

That evening a cool swim in the crystal clear water at a beach just around the point from the yacht harbor seemed to build everyone's appetite for our now-famous spaghetti sauce. We'd been at sea for about nine days and repetitions were bound to creep into the menu. Needless to say all partook of gigantic quantities.

After the evening meal we got ready for the new sporting rage of the Adriatic: Female People Watching, with the international one-ten scoring system. We had just drawn our positions and were ready to give the starting signal when some delightful Americans whom we had met briefly in Split arrived at the foot of our gangway. They were Leonard and Jackie Gross and their two youngsters, Jeff, eight, and Linden, ten. Len was the European editor for *Look* magazine, and his charming wife was an authoress in her own right. We enjoyed their company so much that we invited them to join us for a short cruise to a nearby island to swim and explore for amphora the next day. They very graciously accepted our invitation, and after they left to return to their hotel, we resumed our field positions for the evening sport of girl gazing—now known to the initiated as G.G.

Sleep came late that evening, partially because of an excellent field of selection for G.G. and partially because of a raucous band that invaded the still quiet of the evening with almost guttural howls that some people might interpret as music.

That night was the first time the beachfront lookers committed a foul. Although there is no governing body to enforce the international rules of People Watching and its derivative sport of G.G., there is a code of ethics that few civilized people breach, thus committing a foul. However, a woman of rather peasant-looking stock, resplendent with huge waddling buttocks, low-slung, cow-like bosoms, and a face that would please only a mating four-footed bull, stopped, stared, and with complete vulgarity stuck out her tongue. I was stunned motionless for perhaps ten seconds. By the time I had recovered and lunged for my camera, the cow-like creature—this minus ten in any G.G. score—had fled into the passing crowd. With that rather amusing indignity, we decided to call it a day and headed for dreamland.

Friday, August 12, 1966

We had a little shopping to do the next day and went to the local market at six o'clock in the morning. Anytime we had shopped much after six thirty, we found the best of the vegetables, fruits, and other perishables so well picked over that only the unappetizing dregs were left. Even the bread was still warm in the early morning. If we waited too long to go to the bakery, the bread was cold and already starting to turn brick-like. Milk presented somewhat the same problem: at six it was still cool, at seven it was tepid, and much after eight o'clock it was warm and starting to sour because of the lack of refrigeration.

The other hazard of shopping much after seven was that the older native women attacked with fervor, pushing ahead in line to gain the advantage of a space or two. The only defense from their rude pushing was to push back with equal rudeness and ignore their vocal tirades and insults. Physical violence was beyond them. Vocal abuse was their forte and easily ignored.

Leonard, Jackie, and the two Gross children arrived sharply at 7:30 a.m. Fifteen minutes later we were under way, headed for a nearby island that was supposed to be the refuge of a large colony of naturalists—nudists to the unknowing. Fortunately, I suppose, the naturalists had disappeared, and therefore we spent a lovely morning and early afternoon with the Grosses, swimming, skin diving, and talking in a relaxed, enjoyable atmosphere. Although we scoured the bay for underwater hidden treasurers, we again drew a blank. Pete took the spear gun and ventured forth to a nearby reef. His only kill was a four-inch spotted sand fish that disintegrated when hit by the stainless-steel shaft.

The luncheon spread impressed the hell out of Jackie and Leonard. It consisted of Russian caviar, Danish crab, Italian lobster, pickled vegetables, tuna chunks, fresh lettuce and tomatoes, wonderful condiments, and finally fresh and canned fruits of many varieties. We all stuffed ourselves, and although I, frankly, would have headed for my usual siesta, there wasn't room for all to snooze. I took my courage by the throat and dove into the cool, deep blue water to keep awake.

Leonard had been taking pictures in a very professional manner all morning. He concentrated on Robin and her friend Chris. It wasn't until after lunch that I found out why. While we were lazily swimming into a sandy beach, Leonard said, "Don, I smell a real great story here, but since we're both supposed to be on vacation, I hesitate to even mention it. Further, I wouldn't want to presume on our new friendship and invade your privacy."

I replied that I wouldn't mind and further, that if he could get a story, it would help serve as a record of our "two-and-a-half-nickel" tour. We kicked his idea around and agreed that if he could get the magazine's okay, he could write up our adventure as seen through the eyes of Robin and her babysitting friend, Chris. The title could be "The World's Best Babysitting Job." The more he talked, the more intrigued I became. I even asked Luke what she thought and received an enthusiastic affirmative response.

On our way back to Hvar we discussed the possibilities of their joining us in Athens and spending three or four days with us taking pictures, talking to and gaining impressions from Chris and her charge. Because we had become very fond of Leonard and Jackie by this time, we didn't care whether they did a story or not. They could come and cruise with us anyhow. It was left that they would cable us in Corfu or Athens to let us know what they finally decided.

We dropped these new and delightful friends at Hvar and immediately left for Split. We really had to return to Split to pick up the laundry we had left at the Marjon Hotel and replenish our perishable supplies. One other compelling reason was that the skipper had an attractive widow that he wanted to see again. We moored in the same spot where we had been previously, and after cleaning ship got ready for a short before-supper G.G. session.

It must have been old home week, because no sooner had we fielded the team when a stout, rather portly gentleman bounded up the stern gangway. In broken English, he introduced himself as Andrew Mardesich of 1342 West 19th Street in San Pedro, California. He had emigrated from the nearby offshore island of Vis.

Since he spoke both of the languages with ease—his English was by far secondary—I invited him to be our guest at dinner on shore at one of the local restaurants. In this manner I gained a guide and an interpreter in one fell swoop.

He and his wife were grandparents, but full of joie de vivre. We truly enjoyed their company. They led us to a restaurant where we ordered a potent native wine that was drinkable only when cut at least fifty percent with water. We also were served cold native prosciutto with sweet pickles—truly delicious. This was followed by a native dish of small chunks of barbecued baby pig served with raw chopped onions—just great. Luke had barbecued fish, which she found to be good, although she said she wouldn't go ashore deliberately to have it again.

After dinner we received a thorough guided tour of the city. It was fun seeing this ancient metropolis through the eyes of a returning emigrant who had spent his student years in its environs. We saw an old Greek temple that had been converted to one of Europe's first Christian churches. Also, on the tour we saw all four gates of Diocletian's palace brilliantly illuminated by blue floodlights. All the statues were duly visited, and their background and sculptor's history were told to us. Little-visited nooks and crannies of history, some almost completely darkened, were given our nocturnal inspection. Amusing and fun it was, but it was also late, so we bid Andrew and his wife, Lucy, a good evening at about eleven thirty and fell exhausted into bed, having walked too far and eaten too much.

Saturday, August 13, 1966

The sun poured through the cabin ports to rouse me from a dreamless sleep. We were quickly reminded that we had to face the battle of the mauling masses at the marketplace. We gathered up our woven straw and nylon string baskets and set out in the Zodiac boat across the calm waters of the harbor to land as close to it as possible.

We planned to lay over in some cove away from where we could buy food, so we had to fill up with all the fresh supplies we could. Certain items were of good quality and were good buys, such as tomatoes, cucumbers, figs, and lettuce, if you selected carefully. Other items were risky, such as eggs, bell peppers, carrots, beets, and potatoes. Then there were the items that were just beyond hope, such as watermelon, or any melons for that matter. The bread was good for only one day, grapes were sour, string beans were tough, and the milk was questionable and needed to be boiled. One food item we found to be delicious everywhere we went in Yugoslavia was ice cream. It was different from what we are used to in the States. It was more like a sherbet and came in all flavors.

Two other problems are worth mentioning: taking one's turn in line, which seemed to be a sign of weakness, and prices. Prices were unstable in that with fortitude it was possible to reduce your shopping bill by at least a third, but believe me, it took more guts than I had. I was fearful that I'd get put into a Yugoslavian jail and be left there to rot.

Shopping was a drag, and I was pleased to have survived another bout with the Serbs, the Croats, the Slavs, and all the others as we sailed away to the island of Scedro.

We pulled into a small, landlocked bay on Scedro. At the head of a little cove there was a small but colorful stone house. Its red roof set off the white stone walls that were covered with rambling grapevines interspersed with red and pink flowers.

As we dropped anchor, secured engines, and lowered the Zodiac, we could see a robust woman clad in the traditional native black, scurrying around the house and hurrying to and from a nearby vineyard. We loaded the dinghy with two small bags of flour, two or three kilos of rice, chocolate bars, and some jars of honey. Luke and the skipper rowed to shore in the Zodiac, and I joined the girls swimming to the beach. By the time we had arrived, Luke and the skipper were seated at a small rickety table on equally unreliable benches. The woman, who was at least eighty, greeted me like a long-lost son. Her smile stretched from ear to ear, disclosing her one or two remaining teeth. In universal sign language she thanked me for the supplies and insisted I partake of her meager fare. That consisted of delicious figs, hot, rough, dark homemade bread, sour grapes, and home-smoked sardines.

Unfortunately, we had eaten lunch on board the *Cuhona* on our way to Scedro so we were not hungry. I drank a glass of her homemade wine and frankly can't say it was good. Evidently our hostess saw my face pucker and made me to understand that she agreed that the wine was not good this year. She then rummaged around in the rear of a separate building, her cookhouse or kitchen, and produced a bottle that was dust covered with age. This bottle was from a vintage year and delicious. The sardines that were offered to and accepted by the children were surreptitiously fed to the old woman's cats.

We were joined by a man and woman who spoke German and thus, with the skipper's help, we were able to communicate through a third language. The new arrivals were from Belgrade, and the gentleman was a college professor. The lady with him was his wife even though she appeared to be half his age. Shades of Frank Sinatra!

We left the fine old lady, whose radiant smile and genuine hospitality gave us a restored faith in humanity. Her wants were little, yet her joie de vivre was as great as life itself. This old lady of Scedro Island gave us all a truly delightful human experience.

The next port of call was Korcula, which is on an island closely surrounded by literally hundreds of other smaller and a few larger islands. The town was a typically old village that dated back to early medieval times. It had been almost completely restored and was home to many music and art festivals, befitting the historic setting.

As we pulled into the harbor, we saw a three-masted Dutch schooner of recent construction, probably two or three years old. She was about ninety to a hundred feet in length and had a crew of seven, at least four of whom were Americans. This beauty was named the *Rara Avis* and was registered in Belgium. We did not see the owner and had very little conversation with the crew.

At night they posted a guard on their gangway. He carried a policeman's billy, which was just too much for us. Not wanting to be outdone, we decked Pete in the steward's coat, two sizes too big, and posted him with our pellet gun at the foot of our gangway. Quite an amused crowd gathered while we took pictures of Pete doing his version of the military guard's manual of arms while walking his post in Buckingham Palace fashion.

That evening our culinary efforts were frankly not up to our usual high standards. We were running out of steam or perhaps we were just tired, but we settled for an uninspired dinner of roast beef, canned vegetables, and mashed potatoes. Good, but not great.

We turned in early, hoping for a long night's sleep before our trip to Itok Mljet, the island of amphora. We didn't get it: around eleven o'clock the wind shifted and started to blow upward of forty knots. It was an all-hands situation to which Julie, the skipper, and Tim responded. The rest of us figured the other guy would do it, so we stayed in bed. I guess they didn't need us because they got us off the quay and safely anchored away from shore in the middle of the harbor, where we rode out the storm until morning.

Sunday, August 14, 1966

The bay's surface was mirror smooth as the sun rose over the neighboring mountains and burst into our cabin, making sleep no longer possible. We made a quick run to the market for bread and a look at the local vegetables. Neither were very good, but bread being the staff of life, we had to partake.

By 8:30 a.m. we were under way for the island of Itok Mljet and its hidden cove, which supposedly was covered with amphora. We arrived at that clandestine nook and as soon as the anchor was set, over jumped the skin divers. The skipper was right. In about two minutes Pete came to the surface with a gasp for air. In his hand he had the spout and two handles of the top of an amphora jar. I jumped overboard with fins, mask, and snorkel. Through my faceplate I could see the bottom about twenty feet down just as if I were looking through a clear green crystal. It was littered with jars: the larger, almost complete ones were to be found in about thirty feet of water, and the bits and pieces were in from ten to twenty feet. I was satisfied with the bits and pieces.

Tim and Pete were in much better condition and went for broke. They did very well, and Tim copped the prize with an all-but-complete amphora that he found in about thirty-five feet of water. Actually each one of us found something of interest.

We spent the late morning and early afternoon diving. Our collection became huge so we went through a culling process. We left many treasures for the next guy, but I will admit we kept some really beautiful pieces. We didn't know what we were going to do with them except photograph them for posterity's sake and return the objects d'art to the sea in some other remote bay for future generations to discover.

Late that afternoon, after we had prepared the fixings for beef Stroganoff, Luke and I took the Zodiac and went exploring in the neighboring inlets. This island was loaded with coves and inlets. It was different from the country we had previously visited in that the hills were heavily forested and brilliantly green. Again, I compare it to the northwestern section of the States or even some parts of the coast of Maine.

While poking among these inlets we came across a reef that looked suspiciously like it might have hidden in its crags a treasure of amphora. We marked it for exploration in the morning.

Back on board we prepared the evening repast as the brilliant red sun set into a glassy smooth sea. The Stroganoff was a great success, and only firm commands and dire threats of reprisal saved enough to use with spaghetti at another meal.

That night in a still calm broken only by the soft splash of wavelets against the nearby rocks, we watched the millions of stars that canopied our sky. A satellite rushed across the heavens to bring us back to the amazing twentieth century.

Monday, August 15, 1966

We rushed through breakfast in anticipation of discovering a rare, complete amphora on the reef we had located the previous evening. Pete, Wendy, and Lonnie joined Luke and me in the Zodiac as we putted across the bay, pushed by the world's worst excuse for an outboard, a Seagull. Smoking and choking we pushed through the calm waters to our treasure area. Splash ... kerplunk ... plop ... and splat—we were all in except Luke, who remained on board to captain the Zodiac.

Immediately we spotted a huge jar in an upright position with both handles intact. Pete went down first. When he popped back to the surface, he reported it was a beauty, but he couldn't budge it. I went down, and try as I did, couldn't budge it either. The coral had grown around it and cemented it to the bottom. We even tried to move it by taking a line around it. Nothing worked, so with much reluctance we moved on to hunt for something better. We spotted a twin to the locked-in jar and attacked it. We had the same unfortunate results.

Discouraged, frustrated, and fatigued we headed back to the *Cuhona*. Once on board, our spirits soared, because when we surveyed our collection, we all agreed it was magnificent.

We must have spent easily two hours posing, arranging, and rearranging our treasures while we all played the role of a photographer until we were almost out of film.

Since we had a three-hour run to Dubrovnik, we got under way at three o'clock in the afternoon in order to be moored before nightfall. We passed many inviting islands on the way. We knew we couldn't see everything on this trip, so as we slid by tiny, well-protected coves, safe, well-protected harbors, and small, quaint villages, we knew we could come back someday and still have new unspoiled spots to visit.

We tied up to the quay at Dubrovnik with a Mediterranean stern, to be sandwiched in among the largest collection of foreign yachts we had seen to date. Most of them were Italian. There was one uncommunicative American on a Chris-Craft Conqueror, and I figured that any guy on a Chris that was in as bad a condition as that one was wasn't worth bothering to talk.

The weather was hot and oppressive. All on board felt the heat, and tempers became sort of short and crackly. Dinner was a flop, the baby was cranky, and I was ready to bite everyone's head off. It was also at this delightful time that our first case of tourista trots became evident. We doctored the tourista dancers with Dr. Bob's best patented plugs.

To get away from it all we took the Yugoslavian version of the Toonerville trolley from a station near the quay for about a ten-minute ride over a hill to the old walled city.

This city, once completely destroyed by an earthquake, fire, and a tidal wave, was rebuilt in medieval times and had remained in wonderful condition. There was a constant rebuilding program that rang on first appearance with true authenticity.

Because of the heat, my meanness, and Luke's fatigue, we decided to make a short evening of seeing this wonderful city and returned to the *Cuhona*, leaving a more thorough visit until the next day.

Tuesday, August 16, 1966

The heat was still with us the next morning. We roused the gang out of the hay early, and by sheer orneriness I got them all fed and moving before the morning rush. We boarded the Toonerville trolley by seven fifteen and bumped, rattled, and shook for ten minutes over the hill to the main city gate. Unfortunately, everyone else had the same idea, and before the trolley had traveled three stops, it was hocked full of nuts like us, and the even nuttier were hanging like leeches from the outside.

There were streams of people scurrying like ants in and out of the massive stone gate. Antlike, we followed the rest of the people and were swallowed up into the walls. We rushed around looking at points of interest but not really seeing anything.

Robin fed the pigeons, Laurie and Pete walked the entire wall, and Luke and I couldn't wait to get back to the boat and get to the coolness of the open sea.

By ten o'clock we had corralled all the troops. Wendi and Chris rushed Robin to the ice cream store for a quick tankful of cool stuff before we got under way. Once under way, we felt better. We cooled off and our tempers evened out. All was forgiven; we were at peace again.

We ran on down the coast past some nudist colonies. We gave each group of nudists a thorough inspection and again came to the conclusion that those who shouldn't, do, and those who don't, should—become nudists, that is. However, there was one notable exception to the foregoing statement, but when that livin' doll, at least a number eight, saw us approaching with binoculars poked through all available ports and windows, she discreetly retreated to the cover of the sea right up to her neck. Oh well, you can't win 'em all.

We stopped for a swim off the Riviera-like coastline. The shore was dotted with modern hotels perched high on precipitous cliffs with stairs and elevators running down to the sea. The vegetation was green and lush. Here there were even sandy beaches, a rarity for us so far on this trip. We swam with happiness and contentment. We had cooled off physically and mentally.

As soon as we climbed back on board, we upped anchor and headed for the bay of Kotor. After passing the entrance, which was guarded on each side by huge forts of World War II vintage, we pulled into the northernmost corner of this large bay to anchor about a mile off a sandy beach.

There was quite a wind blowing directly off the shore, so we found it difficult to get in to the teach for an inspection of the feminine pulchritude. Robin, who by now was our most ardent swimmer, delayed our voyage until she had had a sufficiency of bathing. We finally prevailed upon her to rejoin the group, and then we steamed into the majesty of the Kotor Fjord.

This body of water is made up of two large north and south bays, which are connected by a narrow channel. The innermost bay is surrounded by mountains with altitudes of more than five thousand feet. The shoreline is rocky and drops off rapidly to a depth that our fathometer could not register only twenty yards from shore.

Words are really inadequate to describe the massive raw beauty of the scene. Along the route there were many small villages at the water's edge and high on the mountains. Most of the small, complete villages nestled high on the hillside were completely deserted and fast reverting to nature, with trees growing in the streets.

The city of Kotor lies at the extreme southern end of the inner bay. The old city is completely walled and is famous as a maritime community.

Our arrival was heralded by flashes of lightning and a roll of deep, rumbling thunder. We quickly tied to the dock, and the threatening blackness demanded the doubling of all lines. We had time to run to the nearby market to replenish our fresh food supply. Then the storm hit.

It was wonderful. It rained hard, and the wind rushed down the nearby mountains in tremendous gusts and slammed broadside into our dockside of the vessel. It was a magnificent storm. Robin laughed and shouted with joy at each lightning flash and clap of thunder. Since this was her first, honest thunder-and-lightning storm, we were pleased with her reaction.

The storm lasted until well after dark, and for the first time in two weeks we were forced to eat in the salon. Actually, it was fun to be warm, dry, and safe inside while the storm beat against the side of the vessel. Our dinner that evening was again made up of our now internationally renowned spaghetti sauce. Each time we served it, the flavor was more succulent. Julie prepared the salad and by this time was becoming akin to a salad virtuoso. We tapered off this bountiful repast with simple tea biscuits and delicious white wine.

The rain was still falling after dinner, but it had moderated to a steady drizzle. In a way this was a blessing, because the weather remained cool and the drizzle kept the crowds away from the quay. We were thus left in peace. By 9:30 p.m. we had gone to bed, but Tom and Julie walked through the almost deserted town, returning within the hour well pleased with what they had seen.

Wednesday, August 17, 1966

We sounded reveille early the next morning. A challenge was before us that had to be conquered before the heat of the forenoon set in: a mountain to climb and a fort at the top that had to be stormed.

Immediately in back of the town was a steep hill that rose more than a thousand meters up an almost impenetrable cliff. Stairs and footholds had been cut into the cliff. We had been told that the view from that height was well worth the supreme physical effort required to get there.

By 7:30 a.m. we had left the boat. A number of false starts were made trying to find the base of the path that led up the mountain.

Finally we came to an iron gate that was locked with a cheap modern padlock. We guessed we were just too early for the keeper of the gate, so after a very short debate and a scouting foray by Pete, we all climbed over the ten-foot obstacle. We made our way straight for the wall that enclosed the vast area and started to follow it upward.

The ascent became increasingly difficult. Sections of the wall were missing, and thus vertical drops of more than a thousand feet were exposed. One slip and we'd be shouting "Geronimo" without a parachute.

Discretion had to be exercised, and since I was the leader of this foray, I called a halt to the ascent, hoping there would be another, better, and easier route to the summit. We threaded our way back down to the base, where we started on a path that headed upward but in an opposite direction. The going was much easier. The higher we got, the more my age became evident. From leader of the field I retreated to the tail-end Charlie position. Tom, a true gentleman, took pity on my fast-deteriorating condition and waited for me as I paused for breath more frequently. Sweat was running off me by the bucketful. The others reached the base of the old fort that crowned the summit a good hundred yards ahead of me.

Finally, I staggered to the top, where I waited to catch my breath for the final dash and assault on the fort. My respite was brief, but I got my second wind and made the top tower of this deserted, dilapidated, and ruined memento of past wars.

True, the view was worth the physical exhaustion. We had made the climb of nearly five thousand feet in thirty-five minutes. No wonder I was utterly pooped. All the others admitted that the pace of the climb was tiring, but since I had set such a fast beginning, my companions weren't going to slack off along the way.

We stayed on top for perhaps twenty-five minutes, and then came a flying descent. We got down in just under twenty minutes. Not once did we stop—we literally ran down the pathways.

Our reward at the bottom for having completed this historical conquest was a drink from one of the town wells that had the coolest, sweetest, and best-tasting water in all of Europe. For that matter, we went back many times to it during the day to fill all the empty wine bottles we had saved.

Tired but triumphant, we staggered back aboard our sanctuary, the *Cuhona*.

Since we had that ordeal behind us, we insisted that the captain and Tim take Chris up this relatively easy climb to show her the sights. We told them it was little more than a stroll through the park. Convinced that it was worthwhile, they departed.

I tried to follow them up the climb through the binoculars, but I couldn't spot them. Perhaps they couldn't find the path, or perhaps they had made it to the nearest pub, thereby completely outsmarting us. Then I spotted them at the peak. They had scaled the summit.

I was eager for their return so I could learn how they had made it up without being seen. Maybe there was an elevator or hidden train.

They finally arrived back at the boat. I quickly interrogated them and found that they had taken the hard way up, the one we had abandoned. I felt better—at least they didn't get a ride to the top.

After we all recuperated, Luke went out and found a small pastry shop that had been operated in the same location for more than two hundred years. She had Lonnie, Wendi, and Laurie with her, and between the four of them, they tasted everything in the shop. They then placed the largest order in the shop's history. Their total bill, not including fifty cents' worth of ice cream, was just over two dollars. They returned with heavily laden baskets and bags containing the most delectable of the shop's many varieties.

By this time the heat in Kotor was becoming oppressive. We couldn't swim in the town's environs, so we cast off from the dock to search for a quiet cove in which to moor the boat while we swam. Two miles from town we found a modern concrete pier and decided we'd moor alongside.

As we approached the dock, Pete hopped off the boat to catch the mooring lines. At the same time Laurie dove overboard into the invitingly cool waters. Just as Pete caught the first line, we heard a wild shout and looked up to see a green-clad, fully armed soldier charging threateningly toward Pete. We got the message fast. Laurie, in the water, shouted and sang, "They're coming to take you away, ha ha," a takeoff on the record that had recently been released by Napoleon XIV. Pete wasn't going to be taken anywhere, and with a mad leap he shot from the dock and landed twenty feet from the pier.

Once he hit the water, he added another hundred yards in world-record time with kicking feet and flailing arms. While Peter was making good his escape, Laurie was still singing, "They're coming to take you away, ha ha."

After we pulled away from the pier, we anchored a hundred yards from the shore and all dove in for a swim. When we were all in the water, two army trucks filled with soldiers arrived and piled out onto a beach just opposite us. At the same time, about a half mile away, a dirty, ill-kept boat chugged away from a dock. Something was amiss. Perhaps we had inadvertently anchored close to the Yugoslavian Atomic Energy works. Whatever we were doing, it wasn't right, so before anyone shot at us or we were boarded by armed police, up came the anchor and we hauled out of this forbidden territory to make for another cove populated by civilians with happy and peaceful intentions.

There the water was just as cool and just as clean, but somehow it felt softer and more relaxing.

Since we didn't want to steam back to the heat of the city, we remained at anchor in the quiet of the bay. The wind had died, and again the heat seemed to slam down and cover the whole bay. We sat and simmered, losing all incentive to create our usual gourmet dinner.

Julie came to our rescue and concocted a cool and deliciously appetizing salad that hit the spot all around. After supper there was still no reprieve from the heat. Not a whisper of a breeze stirred the surface of the entire bay to relieve our discomfort. We went to bed, but sleep didn't alleviate our misery until the early hours of the morning.

Thursday, August 18, 1966

Each day seemed to start, at least for us, with a challenge, a purpose, or a goal. This dawn brought all three. The challenge was to fight and, we hoped, leave the field of conquest not too badly mauled at the marketplace.

Our purpose was to load up the crew with their favorite ice cream.

The goal was to leave Kotor with pleasant memories and the satisfaction of bringing a little more knowledge to all of us.

I'm happy to report that we accomplished all that we set out to do. The battle of the market went better than we anticipated. We didn't have too much to buy, and actually the products were quite inferior, so we didn't argue with anyone. We capitulated to a few high prices.

After our usual continental breakfast, we turned Luke and the kids loose at the ice cream and pastry shop. They had a ball. They spent and spent. They tasted everything all over again. They beat their record of the previous day and spent three dollars on pastries and one dollar on ice cream. We were confident that the record they set in Kotor for pastry and ice cream purchases would be long standing and difficult to beat.

The maritime museum provided the little bit of extra knowledge. We searched it from top to bottom, every cranny and crevice, to learn more of the background and reason for this little city, which is tucked into one corner of this scenic fjord.

We learned much more than we had expected, including the fact that Kotor was represented in the Great Armada against England. There were ships from Kotor?? the famous sea whalers in the Arctic. All these bits of information helped in the appreciation of our trip.

After leaving Kotor we stopped at the small Island of the Church. The only thing on this man-made island was a beautiful small church with a most ornate gold-and-silver altar mounted on a beautiful Italian marble base.

The island was created when a picture of the Madonna was cast up on a rocky pinnacle during a fierce storm. From then on whenever services were held there, people brought stones to drop into the seventy feet of water surrounding the rock. Over the centuries an island was created, and on it was built this small and beautiful church.

Robin, who had been collecting small stones and pebbles from beaches all along the Yugoslavian coast, dropped them into the water as her contribution to the future.

Our next stop was the small city of Budva, a four-hour trip down the coast. We thought the farther south we traveled, the fewer tourists we would encounter. Wrong again. The place was loaded with tourists. Even the small, out-of-the-way beach where we stopped to swim, just before Budva, was packed. It was at this beach where we met and talked to two well-educated, English-speaking Polish people. Both were men of science and internationally prominent in their respective fields.

Because we talked of many things, including Vietnam, communism, capitalism, segregation, and other controversial subjects, I won't identify them any further. However, I will say that America has a great many friends all over the world. These American friends thought our leadership was immature, hesitant, and without purpose or direction. Further, they thought that we would mature, that there could be a purpose to our policy, and that the near future would show us and the rest of the world that the direction we should take was toward world peace.

All the people I talked with remarked that the Chinese constituted the greatest question and threat to the stability that everyone was looking toward.

Enough politics, enough preaching, but let's keep thinking.

Once moored in Budva, we left the *Cuhona* and did our usual quick sizing up of the town. This town catered strictly to the tourist. There were nightclubs, fancy hotels with cabanas, and every other conceivable tourist attraction, including gambling and girls.

After our quick look-see, we returned on board for another spaghetti dinner made with a chunky meat sauce. Really superb beyond belief.

Dinner finished, we started a more thorough investigation of this tourist trap. Our first impression was correct, only more so. By this time we had had enough of being a tourist attraction, and besides, the harbor smelled. Leaving Tim and Chris behind, since they had left without telling us where they were going, we pulled out of Budva to anchor in the middle of a large adjacent bay for the night. We left them the Zodiac, but little else.

Yes, there was some confusion, but they did finally make it back to the *Cuhona* early the next morning.

Friday, August 19, 1996

We arose to our last day in Yugoslavia. We made a quick but rather unfruitful trip into Budva to try to buy some fresh provisions. We did badly. There was little offered, and the quality was terrible. Bread and milk were our only purchases.

Tom and Pete wanted to buy a souvenir rug or pipe of some sort, but even in this category of junk the supply and quality were limited and the prices far too excessive. They left disappointed, but wiser and richer.

Our first stop after Budva was the island of St. Stephan. This entire island, about two and a half acres, was packed with old buildings that had been converted to modern and well-equipped hotel rooms. A large restaurant built high on a bluff overlooked a blue, well-protected, quiet bay. We swam at St. Stephan for about four hours. The water was cooler than what we'd experienced in the previous days, but it was very invigorating.

Lunch was a catch-as-catch-can meal since we didn't want to fuss with dishes and such before our trip to Bar and our departure from Yugoslavia.?? Because we were going to be under way for seventeen straight hours all through the night, Luke cooked a roast beef that the night watch could eat cold at their leisure with sliced tomatoes, mayonnaise, bread, and anything else they could conveniently lay their hands on. Once the cooking was out of the way, we left St. Stephan.

In two hours we pulled into the modern, well-equipped, but sterile-looking port city of Bar. As we rounded the breakwater, forcing a sudden shift in wind, one of my jumpsuits that had been drying suddenly blew off the stern. I didn't see it happen.

All of a sudden Tom ran to the side and, without stopping, dove off the boat while it was going full speed. My first thought was Robin.

She was safely seated in her accustomed spot. A fast swivel of my head accounted for everyone except Tom. I saw him bob up in the wake and strike out with powerful strokes to something floating in the water. By this time the skipper had chopped the engines and the ship had started to swing, reversing its course.

We recovered Tom and my jumpsuit without further incident, but for a few minutes, things really popped.

Customs, immigration, and secret police, after keeping us waiting for almost two hours, gave us a quick and perfunctory clearance and left the ship with few words and a bon voyage bid.

The wind had picked up to a certain extent, and our course, due south until 3:30 a.m. the next morning, lay across the swell created by the blow. All hands lined up for some Dramamine and then promptly flaked out all over the afterdeck. I stood a watch from 5:00 p.m. until 8:00 p.m. I went below for a sandwich and then ducked down for a few hours of sleep since I had drawn the midwatch. I wedged myself in a bunk and was rocked rather violently at times to sleep.

Saturday, August 20, 1966

The next thing I knew, a not-so-dulcet voice advised me that it was time to go on watch. Shades of the old, old U.S. Navy. I hadn't stood a midwatch for more than twenty years, but somehow it seemed the usual thing to do as I clumsily dressed in the dark. I arrived on the bridge and was given the course, time of next course change, and lights to look for, and then I relieved the watch. Tom was my watch-mate.

We didn't see any of the lights we were supposed to see, but we did see a few we weren't meant to see. Evidently our track was quite a way west of our course, because we were seeing the lights on the Italian coast and none on the Albanian coast. I didn't bother to alter course to compensate because if we were to err, I preferred that it be westerly rather than to the east and toward unfriendly Albania.

We sighted three or four large ships during the night, but all passed well clear of us without incident. I changed course at 3:30 a.m., knowing we were not anywhere near where we should be; nevertheless we were clear of all hazards, and our landfall would be the western shores of Corfu instead of the northeastern shores.

Dawn started to break faintly in the eastern sky when I sent Tom below to wake the next watch. I was tired and quickly apprised Tom, my relief, of the navigation situation and then tumbled into my bunk to fall asleep without even taking off my clothes. I awakened three hours later with the sun shining full in my face. I looked through the port and saw land a mile or so off. Since it was east of the boat, I thought it might be Albania. It was.

We were going through a narrow channel between Corfu, Greece, and the Albanian coast.

The Albanian side was bleak of house and bare of vegetation. Through the binoculars I could see newly excavated gun emplacements. On the Greek side the country was lush with trees, and small villages and farms were scattered as far as the eye could see.

While rolling before the wind and sea through this narrow passage, we were hailed by a small Greek fishing boat and asked for a tow in universal sign language. We swung around, threw them a line, and started off at our usual ten knots. This was too fast for them. We nearly sucked them completely under. Frantic shouting and waving finally got through to us, and under reduced speed we steamed into Corfu.

Upon our arrival we were greeted by a Mobil sign high on a hill that read Welcome to Greece. We knew we were back in the West. The only large illuminated sign we had seen in Yugoslavia was one of huge dimensions that spelled out TITO. I loved the commercialism of it all.

We docked at the customs dock and were immediately boarded by a polite representative of the harbormaster's office. The captain went through all the required paperwork and forms to clear our entry into Greece. Actually, Yugoslavia was much more casual about our entry than Greece was.

As soon as we were allowed, the boys went over to change some dollars to drachmas. They got themselves into the hands of a slick Greek who tried to charge them a prohibitive rate for making change. Tom found a young Dutch girl working in a souvenir shop who gave a much more reasonable rate, and she got our business.

After the money-changing business, Tom and Pete hired two motor scooters, quickly packed their sleeping bags on the rear, and took off to see the island.

The rest of us, knowing the Greek custom for a siesta during the heat of the day, adopted this idea and all stretched out in the shade to catch forty winks.

We finally roused ourselves about four in the afternoon and decided we'd better get some marketing done since the stores and marketplace would be closed the next day, Sunday. Evidently we were too early for the Greek merchants, because nearly all the stores and stalls were shut up tighter than a whorehouse on Sunday, just like the old Greek saying—never on Sunday.

However, we were able to buy a cool drink at a small roadside café.

When we returned to the *Cuhona*, we found the captain chatting with a journalist and photographer from the Belgium magazine *Panorama*, which was equivalent to our *Life*.

We met the gentleman and his wife, Mr. and Mrs. Wilko Bergmans. They were an interesting couple on an assignment to do a story on Corfu. They had noticed the Belgium flag flying on the *Cuhona*'s stern, so they thought they would see if there was a possible story connected with the yacht. After much stimulating conversation, Robin woke up and stole the show. The writer thought she was fascinating, and thought he could form a picture story around her. Who was I to discourage a man of the fourth estate?

We didn't cook aboard that evening, but took most of the remaining crew, except Chris, who was looking after Robin, and Tim, who by this time was attentively looking after Chris, out to dinner.

The spot we picked was a small local restaurant in an alley a half block off the main street. It had the impressive name of Pantheon. Very Greek, very plain, fairly clean—and very good.

Luke's chair was on the alley, and whenever a truck passed and gave a long toot on its horn, she had to pull in her chair close to the table to let it pass.

I had shish kebab that was the best ever. Luke had a fish, possibly mullet, that she said had a strange but delicious taste. The children followed my example and were well pleased with the excellently seasoned lamb.

The wine we had with the meal was a complete bust. I think the communication breakdown, caused by the vast difference in language, caused us to get resinated wine when we asked for wine with no resin. *Nyeh* in Greek means "yes"—so you figure it out.

After dinner we walked through the town. The narrow streets, packed side to side with shops selling almost anything available in the world today, resembled to a degree a Moroccan casbah.

Our wanderings took us to the Greek royal summer palace. From the outside it appeared that a scrub brush and a coat of paint would greatly enhance its appearance.

The most interesting sight connected with the palace was the Royal Guard. They were dressed in white BVDs covered by short ballet skirts. On top they wore bouffant blouses with frilly sleeves and collars. Their heads were covered by a Grecian version of a fez with a black tassel that hung in front of one eye.

Their shoes had fluffy pompoms on the toes that would be great for our gal cheerleaders at a stateside football game.

The guard patrol was unique. The posts were about sixty yards apart—fifty-five meters to be continental. Every fifteen minutes they left a candy-striped wooden box and charged one another at a fast walk. Just before their chests collided head-on, they did a fancy three-step turn, avoided one another by centimeters, and ended up charging in opposite directions.

After reviewing the guard, we had had enough entertainment and returned to the *Cuhona*, tired and ready for the sack.

Sunday, August 21, 1966

I was rather rudely awakened the next morning by a shrieking voice amplified by a loudspeaker. I jumped from my bunk and peered through the porthole. There next to us was a high black wall that hadn't been there the night before. On closer inspection I realized that a huge ocean liner had moored next to us at the quay and that the shouting was connected with the docking of the vessel.

Sleep was no longer possible, so we ate a leisurely breakfast and cleaned up the ship. Again we tried to do some shopping, but it being Sunday, nothing was open except two churches on every block. Since we planned to get under way at noon for Paleokastritsa Bay, we cleared with the harbormaster at eleven o'clock.

As we were preparing to haul the stern gangway aboard, I heard two screeching sets of tires and brakes. I looked up expecting to see a major traffic accident just astern of the boat. It was just two very dusty, dirty, and saddle-sore American men, Pete and Tom. Evidently they missed my cooking and returned to the fold earlier than they had anticipated. We welcomed the prodigals home and cast off for a five-hour trip around the northern end of Corfu.

The wind blew up and the weather became slightly dusty. We supplied those who wanted it with Dramamine, but not many were needed since we were all pretty well getting our sea legs.

The wind picked up to twenty-five or thirty knots as we rounded the northern tip of Corfu, and since it was a southwester, we felt that our best bet was to duck into the first quiet cove we would come to. After about a thirty-minute run southerly down the coast, we came to the first shelter. We ducked in behind a cape and dropped anchor in three fathoms of water that was smooth and protected, although the wind was still howling down the nearby cliffs in unrelenting gusts.

We dove in . . . What a shock! That was the coldest water we had felt in three weeks. Not freezing cold, but enough to make you grab a breath upon first contact. I rowed Robin over to a sandy beach in a tiny cove that barely accommodated the Zodiac. She didn't seem to mind the water's temperature and plunged and played happily.

The wind started to moderate around five o'clock, so we decided to continue our way to Paleokastritsa, which was really only a thirty-five-minute, ten-knot run from our present position.

The sea had calmed down to the point where we had a most enjoyable trip down the coast practically right on the beach, which was nonexistent because of the high sheer cliffs that plunged straight into the sea. There were many offshore small, rocky pinnacles that combined with the cliffs to make this coast a most formidable lee shore to be caught on in a storm.

The bay at Paleokastritsa, the legendary landing place of Homer's Odysseus, was unbelievably beautiful. There were about six small anchorages in the immediate area, only one of which was unsafe in a southwesterly. One of the coves contained fuel and water facilities, which were available from a buoy fifty yards from shore. Four boats moored from the buoy at the same time. The main bay could accommodate about eight to ten large boats up to a hundred feet.

We were lucky because there were only three other vessels moored in the bay as we approached. We took an in-shore position and in addition to our bow anchor, put a stern anchor on the beach under some rocks only thirty feet from our stern.

While our anchoring procedure was under way, Pete disappeared below to reappear, after the hard work was done, bright and shiny as a new penny. He had even trimmed his scraggly beard and the curly hair that had been creeping down his neck. I was puzzled at first, but my guess was right.

During their scooter scurrying around the island, he and Tom had found some female companionship residing in palatial splendor with sleeping bags on a nearby rocky beach. Pete was really beyond containing, so as soon as he could, he took off to collect his gal.

Most of the kids joined Luke and myself for a dinner ashore at a small restaurant within a short shout of our stern. Fortunately, we arrived early, 8:30 p.m., so had no trouble getting a table for six. Julie and Tom weren't with us, so our seating demands were not difficult.

The food was mediocre, the service was worse, and the tables were completely unstable on the uneven ground floor. We were hungry, so we ate everything that was put before us.

After supper we were sitting on the afterdeck, admiring the beauty that surrounded us, when I spotted Pete with three other people at the far end of the beach. I hailed him and invited him to bring his guests aboard. Pete was too much of a gentleman to refuse, and he knew I wasn't going to be happy until I had had a chance to assign a G.G. number to his girlfriend.

Pete arrived on board with not one but three girls. They were English and on a hitchhiking tour of Greece. They all were charmers, one by far the most attractive looking. The other two, although not quite so attractive, made up for it with wonderful personalities and snap-crackly senses of humor. They were students from the University of Manchester who, while traveling, had found a way of living, with honest guile, on forty drachmas per day—about $1.20 per person.

We enjoyed their company immensely, and being sympathetic to their much more pressing "two-and-a-half-nickel" needs, we invited them to join us for dinner the following evening.

Time in their company passed very quickly, and it was almost midnight when they politely excused themselves. All on board tumbled into the hay without persuasion. It had been a long but pleasant day.

Monday, August 22, 1966

The next morning while all were taking a dip in the cool waters of the bay, I discovered a new pastime. I named it C.W., for "couple watching" or "camper watching." This new sport was terrific for the curious in search of knowledge about the baser things in life. The necessary equipment was patience, a pair of binoculars, and a fairly secluded vantage point so the contestant would not be disturbed and the subjects of perusal would not become self-conscious.

Two couples camped high on an adjoining hill would have rated very high on anyone's C.W. rating. They were young, attractive, and completely uninhibited as to dress and actions. I let the captain in on my new sport, and the ship's business was brought to a complete standstill for almost a full hour.

I had to quietly retire from this extracurricular activity lest I be missed and the whole thing be shot down. After all, we planned to be there for two days, and I had the next day to think of.

Swimming in the clear, cool water took up the balance of our morning. It also made us work up a tremendous appetite so that by one thirty, we were ravenous.

Nine of us trooped up one of the surrounding hills to a restaurant that Pete and Tom recommended from a previous visit while on their motor scooting. The waiter spoke French, and we found we could converse with little difficulty. He invited us to meet with the chef in the kitchen to confer at length about our menu. That we did, but at first glance I wished I hadn't. That kitchen was a blooming dirty mess of assorted unwashed pots, stacks of used dishes, and piles of unlaundered table linen. Since no one else in the group seemed to take notice of the lack of sanitation, I placed my order after the long conference with the chef. We then retired to our outdoor, uneven, solid-ground *salle à manger* to await our repast.

The luncheon was fabulous. I quickly forgot about the lack of polish in the kitchen. My dish, which was called Sostrito, was a delectably seasoned piece of boiled beef. The salad consisted of sweet sugarlike tomatoes mixed with tender green peppers and cut-up onions that were as sweet as candy.

The bread was overly hot and smelled of that wonderful bakery essence. Luke had a portion of meat pie called moussaka that disappeared almost before I could steal a bit. It, too, was delicious.

I tasted the shish kebab, which was good, not great, and I also stole some of Lonnie's squid, which was absolutely the best dish of the whole luncheon.

We topped off our meal by enjoying a fully flavored, honey-sweet watermelon that was the best we had had since leaving Venice.

Full to the gills, I was once more taken into the kitchen for a conference with the chef. First he inquired as to how we liked each dish. Then he asked us for our suggestions relative to the food and service. Since he was so congenial and sincere, I didn't have the heart to tell him to clean up his damn kitchen.

Finally we discussed the question of the price. He first listed all we ate, and then he assigned a value. He totaled the long list and I was expecting a bill the size of the national debt. The list was long, but after minutes of computing, the bill came to slightly more than a dollar per person. Not cheap, but a fine value.

I had eaten so much that all I wanted to do was lie down somewhere for my siesta. To do so would have meant adding another inch to my expanding waistline, so instead I steeled myself for a long walk. I compromised on a short one and then a siesta.

In the evening our guests, Angela Ross, Maggie Clarkson, and Judy Parry, arrived promptly at eight. We fixed them all up with a before-dinner snootful of booze so that, regardless of my cooking, they'd enjoy themselves.

Needless to day, I shouldn't have been concerned, because I grilled some steaks and they were really great.

After dinner our conversation ran the complete gamut. I was pleased to see that young English people, just as young Americans, didn't really like, want, or condone any of the extremists in their country. They thought miniskirts, Mods, and Rockers were ridiculous. In those girls' opinions, those kooks were the result of too much leisure for immature, half-witted adolescents. My faith in the up-and-coming generation was greatly restored.

Again, it was close to midnight before the girls excused themselves. Since they had to return to the city of Corfu, where we were going the next day to pick up laundry and a telegram, we invited them to join us.

They accepted and left with Pete as their gondolier, eagerly looking forward to the yacht ride the next day.

Tuesday, August 23, 1966

I crept to my C.W. post early the next morning. While on my way to the flying bridge I noticed that the skipper had already taken his position on the field of play. We exchanged curt and knowing looks as our morning salutation. The game of the day was possibly the most interesting and productive from a lewd point of view. All was going great until the captain let out a long whistle and a shout of "Oo-la-la!" That did it. Everyone else on board wanted to know what the excitement was all about. The only way out of this box was for me to make a flying leap from the flying bridge to distract everyone's attention and change the subject. With a shout of "Big Cuhona!" I hit the chilly water. Cold, but safe.

Once in, I persuaded all the crew to follow. We spent the rest of the morning swimming, diving, and cavorting about. I sneaked a quick peep at my C.W. people, but that diversion was gone.

At 11:30 the English girls came aboard and we cast off to return to the city. This time we took the route that went by the south end of the island. It was different, beautiful, and well worth the extra hour's steaming. The sea was almost flat, the weather warm. We rolled in easy motion southerly, enjoying the high forbidding cliffs interspersed irregularly with tiny pebble beaches and small indentures of inaccessible coves. The water grew noticeably more shallow as we approached the southernmost cape, and for a while I was sure we would scrape the barnacles off the bottom.

Coming around a promontory three miles north of the southern tip, we churned up a good deal of mud with the propellers.

Before our final destination of the day loomed before us, we stopped in waters that were rather cloudy compared with the crystal clear lagoons of Paleokastritsa Bay, to let the English girls wet their tootsies for the last time in Grecian waters.

Our arrival this time at the city of Corfu went practically unnoticed except by three or four thousand U.S. Marines and sailors of the U.S. Navy. We steamed very close to a three-ship squadron so that our loyal, hard-fighting servicemen wouldn't strain their eyes looking at the seven and three-quarters bikini-clad gals we strategically placed about our decks. I really should receive a civilian medal for boosting morale. It was fun to hear the whistles, wolf calls, and miscellaneous remarks that were directed to us.

When I appeared with my bald head and by now full-blown jet black Ghengis Khan beard, the tumult died to a loud roar. I wonder what those poor swabbies and Gyrenes thought when they saw that apparition and his harem.

We moored without incident. The English girls, Judy, Maggie, and Angela, bid us adieu and expressed sincere appreciation for their wonderful day of yachting. We were sorry to see them go, as they were good crew, eager to please, and interesting to converse with.

No sooner had they left than the gals remaining besieged the chef and her assistant with queries about the night's banquet. The decision was easy to make.

We would take everyone, Robin and Chris unhappily excluded, to our favorite old sidewalk restaurant, the Pantheon, where passing drivers look over one's shoulder, to partake of shish kebab.

Tom and Pete rented two motor scooters, so we had our own taxis to haul us the two kilometers to the restaurant. I drove Luke over. I managed to get by without hitting anyone and anything, or better yet without being hit by anyone and anything. I lost a few more precious hairs as well as having a few hairs of my black beard turn white in this harrowing scootering experience. That mode of transportation is for kooks and kids.

The Pantheon lived up to its previous reputation. The food was just great. This time we took a table on the row nearest the wall, thereby lessening the risk of being run over while we ate.

Tom, Pete, Laurie, and I had two complete dinners. Luke had a bottle of St. Elena's wine, which she declared fair to good. The tomato salad spiced with sweet onions and Veda cheese was delicious. The whole dinner, including drinks of lemonade and wine, bread, and extra butter which was difficult to get, came to less than twelve dollars, including tip, for all eight of us. My sentiments: good and cheap in the best two-and-a-half-nickel tradition.

Before returning to the *Cuhona*, we stopped at an ice cream parlor and had one of their specials. This was quite an experience. The master of the scoop wields his instrument with great verve, and after dipping into every container in the joint, emptying varieties of bottles on top, he finally, with theatrical maneuvers, crowns the concoction with two wafers. Then, after careful scrutiny, he pronounces them ready for his patrons. The creations were good, but not nearly as good as the show that went into their creation.

Since Corfu was loaded with American sailors and marines, all orderly under the watchful eyes of hundreds of shore patrol officers, we decided to forgo any further sightseeing and head back for the *Cuhona* to sleep, to rest, to dream of tomorrow.

Wednesday, August 24, 1966

We roused ourselves early so we could get under way for the island of Paxos as soon as possible. After putting on a ton of diesel fuel for seventy-five dollars, filling the water tanks, and clearing with the port authorities, we shoved off under a clear blue sky on a mirror-smooth sea for a small cove on the most northern tip of the small but colorful island of Paxos.

As we left the shelter of Corfu, the wind picked up and started to get some strength and sea behind it. Fortunately, we had left early enough so our arrival at Paxos preceded any really heavy cross sea. The cove in which we anchored was crystal clear, sky blue with a white sandy bottom. It was surrounded with high hills covered with olive orchards. Hidden in the ancient and gnarled olive trees were immaculate, whitewashed plaster houses with red tile roofs. Truly a place of serenity and peace.

Hidden in one corner of this tiny bay was a village of twenty-three stone and plaster houses. The whole village turned out on our arrival, and we could have invited all on board and still had room for a dance.

We rested during the day by swimming in the warm water and hiking in the nearby hills.

Our larder was almost depleted. Ingenuity was now required to keep interest and variety in our menus. For dinner that evening we made do with the last of the roast beef. This we sliced into medallion-size pieces and stewed in a wine-and-brandy sauce. That, together with rice, tomatoes, and green pepper, made up our dinner that evening.

We all went to sleep early in anticipation of a twelve-hour run the next day to the small town of Navpaktos with its two-boat harbor.

Thursday, August 25, 1966

Double disaster struck. The freezer that had been acting up for two days gave up the ghost and quit completely. With it we had to heave the remaining beef, chicken, and famous spaghetti sauce.

The second problem was that Lonnie came down with what appeared to be a severe case of food poisoning. Perhaps our freezer had allowed some food to spoil before we noticed and it had hit Lonnie. She was vomiting badly and had had diarrhea all the previous night. We got half a tablet of Empirin with codeine into her and followed it up with a Trancopal muscle relaxer.

With these two calamitous events to start our day, we left our idyllic little cove for our long run. We pulled into the town of Paxos, which had one of the best small-boat refuges I have ever seen. The harbor had two entrances. The northerly one ran in a very deep and narrow channel between the sharp rising cliffs of a small guard island and the main island.

Shortly after entering, this northern channel made a ninety-degree turn to the right and then another sixty-degree turn. At the second turn it became a true "hurricane hole" protected in every direction. The channel was just wide enough to accommodate two medium-size vessels passing side to side. Continuing on for another two hundred yards the channel then opened onto the main small bay where the southern entrance was guarded by a breakwater. Here the harbor became shallow, but we had no trouble carrying our six-foot draft.

We left Paxos promising to return and more thoroughly explore the island as well as make use of its excellent harbor facilities.

We passed by the island of Antipaxos, where there are reputedly beaches of finely crushed marble sand said to be like velvet to walk on. Here, too, the future demands a visit.

Our next point of interest lay thirty miles southeast. We arrived at the Levka Canal in midmorning and passed through under reduced speed. The canal was dug out of a vast marsh and considerably shortened the distance that would be required to go around the island of Levka. At the entrance we saw a Boy Scout encampment with scouts from more than twenty nations. It would have been fun to stop and chat, but we had another seventy miles to run before dark, so we couldn't dawdle on the way.

About six miles south of the canal we came near the island of Skorpios, the hideaway of the Greek shipping impressario Aristotle Onassis. Moored alongside the island were a few large yachts, but Onassis's dwarfed them all. His was larger than many ocean liners. It was equipped with a helicopter landing pad. Its tenders were bigger than our own ketch, *Little Revenge*. Needless to say, it was exciting to see how the other half lives. The island itself had a few beautiful houses. These small palaces were separated by vast fruit orchards and rolling lawns with bordering flower beds. On top of a hill that crowns the island there appeared to be a building under construction that we thought might be his future palace.

During the day our illness problems were becoming more acute. Wendi came down with the same affliction Lonnie had, and we dosed her accordingly. Lonnie didn't seem to be getting any worse and for that matter, under doses of Trancopal every four hours, stopped squirting from both ends. She still felt weak and had spasms of stomach cramps. We moved her from the stuffiness of belowdeck to a bunk made up on deck. Maybe she wasn't fit as a fiddle, but we thought we were gaining on the stomach problem.

We arrived in Navpatkos just as the sun was setting behind the nearby hills. Immediately in front of us was a small French ketch racing like hell to beat us to the entrance. They won, and as we pulled through the very narrow entrance, I saw their reason for rushing. The harbor could accommodate only two large yachts. If there had been one ahead of the Frenchmen, we wouldn't have been able to enter. We lucked out. We maneuvered to one side of the harbor, dropped our anchor, and then backed across the full width, thirty-five yards, to secure our stern to the quay. We had a full audience watching these maneuvers, and I think we disappointed them by not ramming the wall, the quay, or the Frenchmen.

Julie and Tom, afraid that all the food on board might be contaminated, left us to go sample the food in the town. Little did they realize that I was inspired that evening to cook the tastiest, most succulent, delectable scrambled eggs of my entire colorful career. Along with these eggs, fit only for a royal palate, I heated a very fine Yugoslav canned ham. The dinner was truly a masterpiece of culinary art.

Lonnie had recovered slightly and was enticed by the aroma of my art to eat some scrambled eggs. This, with a few bites of watermelon, she was able to keep down. We decided to turn the owners' stateroom into a hospital ward so Lonnie and Wendi, who was getting worse by the hour, could take over my bunk. I was relegated to sleeping on the cold, hard deck. This I did without reluctance, but I realized that I faced a hard, sleepless night of tossing and turning.

Friday, August 26, 1966

I was right: I hadn't slept much the previous night. My shoulder was stiff, my backside was sore, and my head ached as I struggled off the deck at 6:00 a.m. My plight was of no consequence. The illness problem had improved to a degree in that Wendi appeared to be well on the road to recovery. Lonnie was no better, and we really became worried. We decided to continue on toward Athens. If she didn't improve during the day, we'd call Dr. Maggiodes from Itea and if necessary go straight to Athens for professional medical treatment.

Luke did her shopping at many little specialty stores in the town. I went to the bank to cash a traveler's check. At this office of the Greek National Bank I was subjected to all of the ways and means of how not to treat a customer. First, I was kept waiting for twenty minutes. This I resented because I was the only customer in the damn place. Then when they condescended to wait on me, I was shuffled from one person to another, three times. Upon presenting my passport for identification, signing my traveler's check in the employee's presence, I was kept waiting for another ten minutes while this jerk of a clerk rummaged through some files to see if the numbers on the checks corresponded with the numbers of stolen traveler's checks. I didn't mind the first time he did it, but became quite annoyed when he thumbed through the dirty wrinkled sheets for the third time. I surely missed the service with a friendly smile at the Newport National Bank.

After happily leaving that poor excuse for a bank, I went to a small bakery to buy some gingerbread cookies flavored with aniseed. We had discovered these the night before while doing a quick exploratory trip through the town and found them pleasing to all on board.

Upon returning to the *Cuhona*, I saw that Lonnie seemed to have improved somewhat, so to get liquid into her, we successfully tempted her to eat some watermelon. She perked up a bit after a few bites and proceeded to finish a rather large slice. This good omen preceded our getting under way for the small island of Trizonia, which was on our route to Itea, the port closest to Delphi. By this time the prevailing westerly wind started to get some strength, so we were very happy when we pulled out of the main stream and ducked into a small cove on the lee side of Trizonia.

Here the water was cold at first dip. The wind still blew in great gusts off the island, churning up the warm surface water and exposing the next cooler layer. We all finally made it in, thus revitalizing our energies. We got back enough vim to allow ourselves an overland hike to the one and only village.

On the way to the great metropolis of Trizonia, which consisted of twenty-seven houses, eight bars, and six restaurants, we sampled succulently delicious, fully laden clusters of grapes right off the vine. Maybe the "borrowing" made them taste superb, or maybe it was the thirst from the heat of high noon.

Our presence in Trizonia created quite a stir, and everyone, including the goats, donkeys, chickens, and dogs, came to stare at us. We stared back, not uttering one word—nor did anyone speak to us. The Trizonians won: they outstared us, so we retreated from their sacred soil, beaten at our own game of People Watching.

After lunch and a short siesta, we once again pulled up stakes and made the dash to Itea. Fortunately, the run was straight downwind and we had a comfortable, fast trip.

Itea, the closest port to Delphi, was singularly unimpressive. It was neither new nor modern, neither old nor historical. A concrete pier, to which we moored stern-to, extended out into the bay. Alongside the quay with us were two English yachts. We found out later that both were in trouble. One had taken some ancient treasure from a sunken galleon. By the time the story reached us, the treasure was valued at 9 million drachmas, and the "pirates" had tried to smuggle the goods out of the country but were caught and fined the equivalent of $125,000. According to the naval guard, who was supposed to watch the culprits, the offenders were comfortably resting in the local hoosegow awaiting someone from the British Embassy.

The other English boat had trouble of another sort. We heard the story from an English-speaking shipping agent who told us that after the second English boat had secured to the dock, the Greek port captain helped the Englishman's wife off the boat and perhaps became too helpful or too familiar. Anyhow, the Englishman started to raise hell with the Greek. The Greek resented the refusal of his good intentions and was keeping the Englishman under guard until his pride was healed.

With all this tension in the air, we treaded our way in and around this place very lightly.

Since we had exhausted our supply of meat, we now had to devise meals that were meatless but interesting. For dinner we ate spinach-flavored noodles, along with tomato, pepper, and onion salad. The meal was really better than it sounds, or perhaps we were extraordinarily hungry, because we all scraped every scrap from our plates.

We fell asleep gently rocking to the swell that rolled into this exposed anchorage. We had to get up early the next morning because of our decision to beat the heat of the day on our sightseeing tour.

Saturday, August 27, 1966

Today was D-day. The *D* was for Delphi. We were all up at six. We had our usual trouble getting Chris out of her bunk, but after dire threats she hit the deck. Morning, especially early, is her worst time of the day. She's sort of grumpy and not really worth a darn. I couldn't wait to see her after she was married with three or four little monsters of her own to get going. Nevertheless, we all made it to breakfast and met our two taxis at six thirty. One taxi was a fairly new Zephyr that looked good and ran well; the other was a General Motors museum piece. It was a gaily decorated Chevrolet of late-forties vintage, with a wide variety of colored lights, blessed saints, and taffeta curtains generously distributed inside and out. This car was the "mouse that roared" in that its muffler, well rotted out, gave forth with loud crescendos of exhaust and the pace it displayed was like the fitful darting of a mouse. The black smoke that bellowed from the rear was a free but magnificent touch. I shouldn't have maligned this ancient chariot, because it made the rather heroic climb to the heights of Delphi with a minimum of complaints. I may be wrong, but I thought I noticed the famous ancient Greek charioteer waving a familiar hello as the G.M. masterpiece pulled up to the ruins.

Volumes and volumes have been written by the masters about the wonders of Delphi. As far as I am concerned, it was all understated. I really felt in tune with the magnificence of the past that these stately ruins represented. To view all of the buildings requires a certain athletic agility, because the city rests on a steep hillside, both above and below a modern highway. If we hadn't arrived before the heat, we may not have seen the sights from the heights of the well-preserved stadium to the gymnasium that sits perhaps two thousand feet lower on the mountain.

We did it all despite the fact that we had to carry Robin the whole way. We ended our tour in the museum, which, like every museum, displays its treasures. However, unlike any museum I'd been in before, they charged you extra to use your own camera, and absolutely forbade taking pictures with a person alongside an inanimate object. I practically had a fight with one of the guards when I tried to pose Robin looking up at the statue of the *Charioteer of Delphi*.

We would have liked to stay longer at Delphi, but I had made a deal with the taxi drivers for a special rate if we stayed a specified length of time. Besides it was getting hot, so we left having seen practically everything. I, for one, however, was willing to return to savor the grandeur of the place.

We left slightly behind the other taxi because Chris was still operating on only two cylinders and walked more slowly than the rest. We waited for her and as a result had a wild ride down the twisting turns and cutbacks on the narrow mountain road while our driver tried to catch the car that had left earlier. It was a proud and satisfied chauffeur who dropped?? back at Itea. He had caught his compatriot and thereby displayed his superiority. Me, I was scared all the way, thereby displaying that I was chicken.

As we approached the pier, we saw that a new and beautiful yacht had arrived. She was the three-masted schooner *Carita* of Monrovian registry. Easily 120 feet long, she was Dutch built in 1963. According to the information that flitted elusively around the quay, she was now owned by one of the great Greek shipping tycoons and was the largest sailing yachts in the Mediterranean. Seeing this lovely sailboat in all its sumptuous luxury was a rare and appreciated sight that was fast becoming even more unique in this world of higher taxes and fewer rich.

Before leaving Itea, Pete negotiated with the local English-speaking shipping agent to procure a water-skiing boat with a driver. It cost 120 drachmas an hour, so Pete worked out a short rate for fifteen minutes. Even though the motor was barely strong enough to pull Pete out, we saw them perform for all the locals and waiting ferryboat passengers. The fifteen minutes stretched to thirty. We retrieved a water-soaked, tired, and slightly poorer "Pedro" before we took off toward the Corinth Canal.

After an hour of steaming from Itea, the wind started to blow with a good force 8. The going became very uncomfortable, so we decided to duck into the nearest protected cove we could find. This wasn't as easy as we first thought it would be. Although we found a shore that was protected from the large sea that was building, we were still exposed to the howling gusts that ripped down the mountains in furious onslaughts. We were in a large bay and kept working our way along the shore in search of a place out of the wind. At last, after more than ninety minutes of searching, we pulled into a delightful refuge. We cut the motors and prepared to drift up to our anchoring spot.

Suddenly the bow swung, the motors gunned, and we picked up speed. I ran to the deckhouse to see the captain pointing to the water. Following the direction in which he pointed, I saw the surface of the cove covered with thousands of brown, undulating, ugly jellyfish. This sort of put us in a jam. We either fought the fish for possession of the cove or went out to fight the rising wind while we searched for another refuge.

The wind sting was the lesser of two evils, so we swung back out into the now roaring sea, where the tops of the eighteen-twenty-foot waves blew off into a hard, sandlike spray. Twice more we had to surrender to the jellyfish. Finally we pulled into a bay that had five or six large ship-mooring buoys placed in its most protected corner. We were about to secure to one of these when we heard the now familiar shouts of anguish. We had stumbled into a naval reservation, and the Greek marines on shore were warning us to get the hell out. This was old stuff to us since we had been intimidated by experts in Yugoslavia. Nonchalantly we drifted through their sanctuary and dropped anchor on the other side of the bay off the small dusty town of Andikira. We were reasonably sheltered from the wind, but there was little else to recommend about this spot.

Later in the afternoon Luke, Pete, and Wendi went ashore to do some shopping. While they headed for the one fruit store, I waited at the quay in the Zodiac. The town children gathered to look me over and took turns shouting "Hi" to me. I answered each salutation in kind. It became a game: me against forty children ranging in age from five to twelve.

I was rescued from this losing ordeal when a man dressed in a white, immaculately pressed uniform approached and asked in sign language for the ship's papers. Since all I had on was a bathing suit, I offered to row him out to the *Cuhona*, where he could have a full-blown conference with the captain. He didn't hesitate and jumped with alacrity into the Zodiac. Then, in a Nelson-like pose that befitted his snazzy uniform and obviously great rank, he allowed himself to be conveyed to the *Cuhona*.

Evidently the skipper made short work of the "admiral," because before I knew it, back came his lordship to his lofty spot in the Zodiac. I rowed him ashore.

By the time he reached the quay, he had a very impressive audience to which he was displaying all his talents. As I reached the quay, he took a tremendous jump to clear the water between the boat and dock. He missed but caught himself quickly. He suffered one wet white shoe and a slightly deflated ego. I just sat there awaiting his wrath, but all I got was a disgusted look from his lordship and quiet smiles from his audience.

Dinner that evening was one of Luke's real masterpieces. I couldn't take any credit for this excellent meal, which consisted of eggs Benedict made with fried instead of poached eggs, bacon instead of ham, and genuine honest-to-gosh Hollandaise sauce. Luke was a true magician of the galley to produce that meal.

Only Tom and Julie wanted to go ashore that evening for a walk. Luke and I had expended our energies swimming in the not-too-clear water before dinner, so we had lost our desire to explore. Besides, we had walked the one street, which held no further interest for us. The rest of us remained on board to curl up with good books before sleep.

Sunday, August 28, 1966

The bay was glossy smooth when we awakened in the morning to rush without haste for our swim. Since it was Sunday, the town was stirring only slightly. The church bells pealed with a raucous resonance that I'm sure was intended to jar the local parishioners right out of bed. The bells served one purpose. They caused us to hurry out of the bay to put us on the way to Corinth for a passage through the famous Corinth Canal.

Our passage across the gulf was easy and smooth. The only incident worth mentioning was when a small Greek patrol boat pulled up alongside. The sailors, including the helmsman, were giving us a thorough once-or-thrice-over with their binoculars when they almost collided with us. Their first reaction was to cuss us out, but when we pointed to the wake of our two vessels, it clearly showed that their curvy trail had veered and then lunged toward ours. We felt very sanctimonious as we saw the Greek captain turn on his crew in righteous rage. I wouldn't squeal on the stalwart man of the sea, but he was a most ardent binocular wielder while looking at our bikini-clad decks.

We arrived at Corinth to find the canal closed for repair. A small boat came over to us, and the people aboard indicated it would be open in one, maybe two hours. Since it was only eleven o'clock in the morning, we decided the best way to pass the time was to go to the nearby city of Corinth to stretch our legs and give the city a once-over.

Our combined opinion of the dusty village of Corinth was that it wasn't worth the once it took us to go over. Of course, being Sunday only a few bars and restaurants were open. We couldn't buy any fruit or vegetables, so we settled for yogurt, jam, and some Greek pastries, which we bought in one of the local bars.

By one o'clock we had returned very happily to the *Cuhona*, ready to transit the famous canal of Corinth. We arrived at the west entrance at one thirty, all set to go. The red flag indicating a closed canal was still flying from the yardarm. In the canal itself, a dragline dredge was still loading a rusty, decrepit barge. We pulled off and lay hove to about a half mile from the canal entrance. The afternoon wind started to rise. By three o'clock we were still waiting and wallowing in the now rising sea.

We were getting very frustrated. We decided to have a betting pool as to when the canal would open and let everyone select their own time, thus gaining an additional expectancy to our waiting.

Wendi, age thirteen, won. She guessed 3:20 p.m. At 3:18 the red flag came down and the blue, all-clear flag was raised. At 3:23 we entered the canal.

Our passage was quick. The canal itself represented a fantastic feat of engineering and construction even in today's age of bulldozers and giant earth-moving equipment. To start this project in ancient times with little more than unlimited slave power was an indication of the ambition of the ancient Greeks.

The passage became very narrow and the walls rose vertically on either side, so I gained the impression that we were steaming full speed in the bottom of a deep well.

Not all the surprises were those of the canal itself. The biggest jolt was finding that the day of the highwayman was not dead. In Greece they've just legalized him and given him the name of toll collector for the Corinth Canal.

We transited the length, less than three miles, in about twenty minutes. Our vessel was eighty-three feet long and weighed about fifty tons. There were twelve of us on board. There were no locks, electric mules, or pilot on board. The bill was about forty dollars!

In comparison, three years before on our *Little Revenge*, we had transited the Panama Canal with a pilot through all the locks with the gracious and cheerful assistance of the Panama Canal Company for a fee of eighteen dollars.

Our consensus was that the Greeks no longer needed U.S. foreign aid, just one or two more canals.

We left the Corinth area unhappy because we had been taken. Since we had no definite schedule to get to Piraeus, we decided to lie overnight at anchor away from the heat of the city. We pulled into a protected cove ten miles from our destination and luxuriated in the warm wind that blew with good force off the now green and rolling countryside.

Dinner that evening consisted of a special *soup de la maison*, which was a chicken broth, delicately and masterfully seasoned, to which a box of tiny Italian pasta was added—delicious. We crowned this meal with a famous Salad A?? Lucy et Julie. This consisted of all the cold leftover cooked vegetables, to which Julie added her magic dressing and liberal amounts of finely chopped bacon. The main ingredients of the salad were boiled potatoes, string beans, and peas. When mixed together with dressing, the prime base of which was mayonnaise, then chilled for two hours in the "fridge," the taste was absolutely superior.

As usual when we were anchored in a quiet cove, there was no activity after dinner but a few card games, a chess game in one corner, and a group in the main salon who were catching up on their letter writing. I wrote a few pages in my chronicle and then gladly sacked out.

Monday, August 29, 1966

As we awakened early with a good eight hours of sleep behind us, the crew was all for getting the show on the road to Athens. As we approached Athens, I believe we saw one of the world's few graveyards for old, unusable ships. There were literally hundreds of rusty hulks, some appearing to be of pre-World War II vintage, lying at anchor and deteriorating in the weather. It was a sad sight to see these former queens of the broad oceans lying there, rotting and forgotten.

We pressed on through a large and more active fleet of modern ships. Compared with any port we had previously visited, the activity in the commercial shipping part of Piraeus was fantastic. All the shipping greats, including Onassis, Nacarios, and others were represented with huge fast tankers, freighters, and tremendous bulk carriers. We felt insignificant in our little eighty-three-footer, steaming past, around, and out of the way of these giants.

To the east of the main harbor we found the yacht harbor. Here again we felt like little fish in a big pond. There must have been more than fifty yachts of a hundred feet or more lying at the quay. Nevertheless we steamed into this ostentatious display of the world's wealth just as if we belonged there.

We had looked forward to Piraeus because it was our main mail drop. We weren't disappointed. Letters were awaiting us from the Creccas, Bill Eilers, and my mother, and a cable from George Woodford. We picked this all up at the Royal Yacht Club of Greece.

I must say that we had never been more welcomed in any yacht club in the world. The club itself, a modern white building beautifully furnished, sat high on a bluff overlooking the eastern approaches to Athens. From its broad terraces the majestic beauty of the Acropolis stood out above the skyline of the city.

We caught up on our shopping at a small store near the end of the quay. The shopkeeper spoke English and seemed eager to please. He allowed us to sample many of the foodstuffs before we bought. What he didn't have in his own store, he sent for pronto.

I took Luke, Lonnie, and Wendi to the Athens Hilton so they could get their hair cut, set, and whatever else happens in those places of beauty. They struck out because the masters of the mop were on siesta. I went to the barbershop, where I was more successful. I had a haircut and shave. Because I had grown a black beard for the previous four weeks, the barber spent twice the time trimming my beard than he did cutting the hair on my bald head.

Since we had a dinner date that evening with Leonard and Jackie Gross, we rushed back to the *Cuhona* to get the rest of the crew set for their evening meal. Tom was down with the flu bug, so Pete and Julie, acting as joint chefs, had to prepare for only seven with?? cooking.

We met the Grosses at the King George Hotel in downtown Athens. This hotel was a landmark of hospitality. The rooms were splendid and the service up to traditional continental standards. Although we did not eat there, we understood that the food was excellent and certainly worth trying. A restaurant on the seventh floor with a terrace facing the Acropolis allowed for viewing and stuffing simultaneously.

Len, Jackie, and their children, Linden and Geoffrey, gave us one of the finest presents we've ever received: an onyx chess set in two handsome shades of green and brown. The set was handcrafted by Florence artisans and destined to occupy a prominent place in my office.

After the presentation of this truly wonderful and greatly appreciated gift, we met one of the world's great artists, Tony Vaccaro. Tony is renowned for his photographic work for such magazines as *Flair*, *Venture*, *Life*, and *Look*. The week before we were introduced to him, he had had ten pages of photographs in *Life*. After a short discussion I also learned that Tony had many other talents, not the least of which was gourmet cooking.

Since Tony had been in and out of Athens almost every week for the previous twenty years, he acted as our guide and selected our dining place that evening. He took us to one of the finest restaurants in Athens, the O Geros Toy Marna, in the old section, which is on the southwest side of the base of the Acropolis.

We let our guide order all our food and were very pleased that we had. The menu consisted of different appetizers for everyone, such as succulent marinated octopus, well-seasoned sardines covered with olive oil, moussaka meat pie, a pancake of fried eggplant, and a large order of seasoned crisp Greek salad.

We then ordered our entrees, which we swapped around. Luke had vine leaves, excellent; Leonard had cold shrimp, superb; Tony had a veal-and-eggplant stew, good; Jackie had lamb chops, excellent; and I had shish kebab, good.

After dinner we enjoyed one of the outstanding highlights of our trip: a walk on the Acropolis through the Parthenon in the light of a full moon with Tony as our guide. We were very fortunate, because the Acropolis is open only three nights a month when the moon is full. To me, it magnified all the senses of awareness. The Parthenon seemed bigger, the temple of Diana more beautiful. The lines of the mammoth pillars, columns, and arches softened in the moonlight.

It was in this inspirational atmosphere that I discovered I was in the company of two true philosophers, Leonard and Tony. I should have kept my big mouth shut and listened more. They were tolerant of my opinions, even though I loused up their thought-provoking discussions by putting in my own ill-considered words.

We were the last to leave the Acropolis. The myriad of guards, there to protect the property and discourage rejected lovers from jumping from the parapets, ushered us from this moonlit splendor as a shepherd would herd his goats. To me it was an unwarranted and unnecessary climax to a memorable evening.

Tuesday, August 30, 1966

Since we didn't return to the *Cuhona* until after 1:00 a.m., we slept late the next morning. I didn't get both feet firmly planted on the deck until almost 7:15. Even at that I must admit it was a struggle, but that day required changing money at the bank and shopping for provisions, and, most important of all, was the day Patti and her friend Chris Miller were to join our little, fast-expanding group.

The battle of the bank was even more discouraging than any previous encounters. I'm sure every client of a Greek banking institution must feel the guilt of a common criminal when he walks into the cluttered, crowded, unattractive, and unclean premises.

Again, I was shoved from counter to counter and person to person. I wanted to cash two hundred-dollar traveler's checks. I handed them, along with my passport, to a clerk who immediately dropped my vaccination certificate on the floor without bothering to pick it up. After some conversation that led to some shouting on both sides, he condescended to pick it up.

He then told me that two hundred dollars was too much at one time. I proceeded to explain that it was two hundred I needed, two hundred I wanted, and two hundred I was going to get, either there or elsewhere, and besides it was none of his damn business how much I wanted.

At this point the manager intervened. He gave me the usual suspicious once-over, decided I was reasonably presentable, then put his initials to the traveler's check and without ceremony, nod, or smile, departed. Then I was sent to another counter where they juggled a calculator to determine how many drachmas I was going to be allowed for my dollars. I was given a slip of paper written in Greek, told to sign it, and then ushered to another counter, where I waited while they repeated the exact calculating process again.

The slip of paper I signed was taken from me, along with my passport and traveler's checks. Now I was helpless and worried. I followed all my papers back to the manager's desk, where another suspicious look was cast on me and another initial affixed to the papers.

By this time I was convinced I had robbed a bank, abducted a beautiful girl, and was part of a Greek gang of hoodlums. I could now think only of escape. I reasoned that if I fled now, I'd be caught; if I brazened it out, I could get the dough and still make my getaway. I became crafty. I slunk to three or four more positions. I finally cornered the guy with the dough and was about to push a note to him saying, "This is a stickup—give me my two hundred dollars."

He spotted my evil intent immediately and shoved me the two C's worth of drachmas without protest. I looked him in the eye as if to say, "Keep quiet for ten minutes, buddy, or I'll blow your Fiat up with a cherry bomb."

I breathed a huge sigh of relief as I fled with the hot money and passport papers clutched in my cold little hand.

With Luke as my accomplice, we headed for our provisioner to swap some of our ill-gotten drachmas for food. Once again our little man at the provision store made us forget our earlier trials and tribulations. He exuded charm and graciousness. He was eager to please, and I didn't care if he charged me double the going price—at least I was enjoying it. We didn't have to plan any complicated menus for that day, so our shopping list consisted mainly of staples such as bread, milk, fruit, and vegetables.

Len and Jackie Gross and their two children came on board for lunch. It came from cans, but expensive cans such as caviar, salmon, prosciutto, crab, lobster, and other delicacies that made our table the envy of the quay. Our guests paid us a great compliment in that nothing was left to discard to the fish.

During and after lunch when Tony Vaccaro joined us, Len gave us his thoughts about the story and the suggested title "Baby Sitter's Bonanza." Tony quietly sized up the situation, and I could see he was planning his approach to the photographic part of the story. After this problem was solved, we tackled the most serious question before the committee: "What shall the menu be?"

The discussions were long and intense. Many factors had to be taken into account, such as available refrigeration, size of oven, number of people, and so on. After all, we had to feed nineteen people for three days. That's no small logistics problem. Consensus decided that a few large whole fillets of beef would answer the problem—served first hot, then cold.

By the time we had concluded our meal planning, it was time for Pete and me to go to the airport to fetch Pat and Chris Miller. We caught a cab and after serious negotiations arrived at a price for a round-trip to the airport plus any necessary waiting. I was pleased with my ever-improving negotiating ability. I knew I was being taken, but I was enjoying it more while being taken for less.

We arrived at the airport fifteen minutes early and discovered that the plane was only ten minutes late. This pleased us no end, but our pleasure was short lived. Ten minutes just doesn't mean six hundred seconds to a Greek. We were still pacing back and forth forty minutes after scheduled arrival, wondering worrying thoughts. I must have checked three times with the British European Airways flight operations, and each time I was assured it was only ten minutes late. I was almost panicky but felt a flood of relief when I heard, since we couldn't see the field, the whine of jet engines descending to a stop.

The crowd outside the arrival room was the usual pushing, shoving, undisciplined horde. I just pushed and shoved with the best of them. Finally I spotted Pat. She didn't recognize me at first because of my now pronounced and beautifully coiffured black beard. When she finally penetrated my disguise, her hand flew to her mouth in disbelief.

She then turned away, hoping the apparition would disappear. Next she grabbed Chris Miller and hurriedly whispered a warning to her so as to soften the blow of meeting. I must say that both of them had adjusted to my disguise quite well by the time they burst through the customs barrier. Patti still recoiled slightly. Chris at least gave vocal approval.

Our return to the *Cuhona* was filled with snatches of reports on their wonderfully adventuresome summer. I can't recount their adventures here because they should tell their own story, and besides it would only further confuse this chronicle. Pat was welcomed with effusion by her sisters, and needless to say, Robin showed the greatest enthusiasm for her return. As usual, with her great thoughtfulness, Patti came loaded with gifts for them. Robin received a beautiful doll from Austria, Julie a woolen jacket from Scotland, Laurie a suede leather jacket from Spain, Lonnie a collection of gold charms from various cities, and Wendi a cashmere wool sweater from England.

That evening we let the older kids go to Athens on their own to duplicate our experiences of the previous evening. We were joined by the Grosses and had dinner at a bayside restaurant in the old port of Piraeus. Since our excellent dinner was almost a duplicate of our fare the night before, it would be redundant to describe it. However, in addition to our other delights we had grilled fillet of sole and boiled langouste. We had selected our fish and lobster before they were cooked from a drawer filled with crushed ice.

We parted after dinner, the Grosses returning to Athens and we, with a very tired and cranky Robin, to the *Cuhona*. I was tired, but no sooner had my head touched the pillow than I heard a tremendous commotion on deck.

Wednesday, August 31, 1966

The noise was followed by the thunder of feet across the deck. I pulled the pillow over my head, hoping that whatever was happening would go away. It didn't. Then there was a knock on our cabin door. I answered reluctantly and Julie appeared to inform me that Tom had fallen down the after-companionway and was bleeding profusely from a cut on his head. That was all I needed, a casualty to care for.

I made my way aft to find Tom standing and swaying while holding a piece of gauze to the side of his head. He had suffered a deep gash on the upper portion of his ear. I washed it and put disinfectant on it and then a pressure bandage. I gave him a pain pill and told him to go to bed because I was tired and didn't want to be bothered again that evening. I'd make a great physician. I returned to bed, took two sleeping pills, read a book, and finally fell into a drugged sleep.

The Acropolis, the Parthenon, and the Royal Museum were our objectives for the day. We left the boat at 7:30 a.m. to meet with Len and Tony at the Acropolis at 8:00. Again, we negotiated with two cabdrivers and piled twelve of us into two cabs for the dash to the city. Every time we rode in a Greek taxi, it was a dash, never a ride. We arrived at the base of the Acropolis on time and were even inside the entrance gate before Len and Tony.

Robin had brought her new doll, which occupied her interest far more than the historic surroundings. I think this was just what Tony wanted, because Robin wasn't stiff and posed. Chris, who still didn't know she was one of the central figures of the article, was natural and relaxed. I watched them shoot a few shots at the statue of Zeus that to my amateurish eye were spectacular. Robin folded quickly, and we had to carry her from the history-laden halls in our arms. Fortunately, there were plenty of taxis available to haul our crew back to the boat. I negotiated a maximum charge for each of the taxis, a most necessary ritual because if you don't, you may end up buying a car.

Robin slept all the way back to the boat. Luke and I stopped at the provisioners to restock the ship and add supplies to accommodate our guests, the Grosses and Tony Vaccaro. I wanted to lay in some meat, but Luke kept discouraging me every time I'd mention it. We arrived back at the boat well stocked but meatless.

Len and his family arrived shortly after we did, without Tony. They threw their gear on board and left almost immediately in the same taxi in which they had arrived. I thought something was fishy, but trying to be a good host, I refrained from any inquiry. Nevertheless, I was saddled with their kids and began to wonder what I had let us in for.

About twenty minutes later the same taxi pulled up to our stern and out piled Len, Jackie, and Tony, each with a hand on a large, long package wrapped in plain white paper. On closer inspection the paper appeared oil stained and seemed to emit steam or smoke.

With steady tread and great ceremony they climbed the gangway, advanced across the afterdeck, and solemnly placed the parcel on the dining table. Then they stood back, beaming, and invited me to remove the shroud.

I felt like it was my birthday. I ripped the paper aside and exposed a whole hot roasted or barbecued lamb. The aroma was tantalizing. I slipped a knife from my pocket and sliced a piece to taste. The flavor was rapturous. The sight was fit for an artist's brush. Unbeknown to me, Luke had prepared all the accoutrements to go with this fantasy of flavor.

They then proceeded to load the table with raw, sliced, honey-sweet onions; deliciously tender green peppers; red-ripe, flavor-filled tomatoes; cheeses; bread; and the wines of the country, which altogether created a picture of Louvre-like quality.

I was hungry and ready to dive in, but was forcefully restrained while Tony recorded the feast on film from all angles until his artistic eye was satisfied. They finally unleashed me and I dove in right up to my shoulders. It was fabulous.

There were nineteen of us on board, including the crew. The lamb weighed perhaps forty pounds. At the end of the luncheon there was only half left for the next two meals. We all had a sufficiency.

We were so stuffed with food that it was difficult to move, but we roused from our torpor to go through the motions of casting off and directing the skipper to take us to the island of Hydra. As if in a well-directed play, we all then collapsed in the most convenient spot to sleep off our food orgy.

Five and a half hours later, perhaps an hour before sunset, we arrived at the very colorful town of Hydra on the island of the same name.

We pulled to the quay, hopped off, and headed into one of the many tourist trap shops. The guy we encountered was one of the world's best salesmen. If I'd had any money, he would have sold me his shop, his town, and his whole damn island. Fortune smiled on me, because he cleaned me out of only two hundred drachmas.

We then proceeded to a local gin mill, where Tony and I enjoyed a wee drop of the Greek national drink called ouzo. If one likes a sweet licorice taste, this drink becomes very palatable, and two or three of them are deadly. Fortunately, I stopped at one, and even just one made me feel lightheaded.

In the meantime our boat had been kicked from the quay to make way for three or four tourist-laden inter-island boats, including a hydrofoil of gigantic size.

Since the tourists, including ourselves, seemed to be inundating the town, we felt it best to make room for the money-spending variety. Tim rowed twice to the quay to ferry all of us back to the *Cuhona* so we could get under way for a small cove six or seven miles down the coast. Our arrival was singularly unheralded. Other than a few palace-size houses on the shores and surrounding hills, the area was completely vacant. We saw no one stirring. This was just what the doctor ordered, because we needed a night away from bright lights and crowds.

Dinner that evening was perfunctory. We ate just enough salad and bread to take the edge off a habitual hunger. All of us were tired and sick of looking at one another, so the suggestion of bed was rejected by none.

Thursday, September 1, 1966

For the first time since we had boarded the *Cuhona* in Venice, more than four weeks before, the morning sky was dark and threatening. This didn't change our rule of no swim, no breakfast. There was no mad dash for a dip, but we all managed to dunk enough to wet our heads and fulfill the word of the law.

Then the skies broke open and the rain gods were determined to give us our month's allocation of wet in one hour. We all huddled in the lounge to hold a planning council. Tony's suggestion of visiting the island of Spetsai and the possibility of meeting some of his friends was unanimously accepted. The skipper, always a man of action, jumped at the chance of movement, and we were under way in record time.

The rain had moderated and the sea had lost its angry look, so we ventured from our protected cove to brave the dangers of the deep. The farther we advanced toward Spetsai, the nicer the weather became. As we came close to our destination, the skipper pointed out M. Nicarcos's private island kingdom. We steamed into the harbor of this idyllic hideaway convinced that even the world's billionaires play at keeping up with the Joneses. Nicarcos had a beautiful house set in a huge garden atmosphere. Scattered away from the main house were guest cottages that in themselves reflected a sumptuous fulfillment of good taste. Across this island of approximately six hundred acres, well-paved and well-maintained roads wove a pattern of accessibility. The harbor was sheltered by an extensive man-made breakwater. Lying by the quay was a large, lovely, three-masted, black-hulled schooner that rivaled in beauty any vessel I had seen on our travels. We steamed close enough to see armed guards begin to take defensive positions against an unwanted landing. We were old hands at knowing where we weren't wanted, so, satisfied at just looking, we departed without creating any incident and without a shot being fired.

Spetsai was only minutes away from Nicarcos's island paradise. We steamed into a lovely Greek harbor that adjoined a picture-book Greek town. The sun had now broken through in the west to accentuate the white town, which was offset by a background of heavy green foliage. The storm had disappeared to the east, leaving an aura of calm and tranquility.

The only curious happening was a sudden swell that entered the harbor with quite some intensity. The water remained high for perhaps two minutes, and then the harbor started to drain with what seemed to be a strong tidal current. I jokingly said that if it dropped much more, I was heading for the hills, because it would mean a seismic tidal wave. It didn't reach dramatic proportions, but nevertheless I was a bit nervous.

As it turned out, they had had an earthquake of serious proportions in the Peloponnesus, only thirty miles away. There had been major property damage, many injuries, and some loss of life. Our fate had decreed that we were spared the force of the earthquake, which was felt by all on Spetsai.

We formed an expeditionary force soon after we had secured to the quay in the harbor that lies about a mile east from the center of the town. The troops easily negotiated the walk to town along a paved esplanade. Robin delighted in scaring me by skipping along the sea wall. We scouted out the necessary shops so that in the morning we'd have little difficulty locating the food we would need to buy.

The highlight of our trip to town was eating small portions of shish kebab that were prepared by curbside vendors on charcoal barbecues. Even though we had had tea earlier and it was too soon for dinner, we all had one or two of the temptables. We were even bolder when two of us shared what appeared to be the Greek version of a pizza. It consisted of highly seasoned lamb slices served between the folks of a disc-shaped piece of fried dough. I would have had two more myself and given up dinner, but I caught a quick dirty look from all the kids when I suggested it.

While we were sampling some of the good specialties, Tony met a friend from one of his previous visits, Baroness Roxanne de Hurter, and wangled us a visit to her very interesting house. He arranged for us to be there at 10:30 a.m. the following day.

On the way back to the *Cuhona* we stopped by a quay-side restaurant and in our nonexistent Greek, arranged reservations for fourteen, ordered what we wished for dinner, and, most difficult of all, arranged the table we wanted where we wanted it.

Back on the boat we arranged a simple dinner of spaghetti and cheese for the five or six who wished to remain on board. The rest of us washed and in general made ourselves more or less presentable so we could dine out in style.

The dinner that night was a real ball. We had ordered practically everything on the menu so that each person who had something different would share it with his or her fellow diners. This meant that plates were being passed back and forth like flying saucers. No sooner would I have my fork raised to spear a particular succulent piece of squid or octopus than whoosh, the plate would move and I would spear thin air. However, I must admit that I created my share of misses of morsels. In all there were fifteen of us at the table, so between our passing plates and the waiters bringing new ones, the dinner could only be classified as a meal of first-class commotion, confusion, and fun.

The hilarity lasted until we returned to the boat. We joined in the Greek spirit of things and sang songs while we strolled through the streets. No one paid a bit of attention to us, as this was not at all unusual for those music-loving people. It was a happy, weary crew that shuffled rhythmically aboard. Frankly, I didn't even stop on the afterdeck but just danced my way right into bed.

Friday, September 2, 1966

A tour for supplies was the first order of business. Len and Jackie joined Luke and me for the trek to town. It was a glorious morning with golden bright sunshine piercing a contrasting dark blue, cloudless sky. It was great to be alive, in Spetsai, with family and friends. Nothing could spoil our joie de vivre, so I didn't bother to argue with any of the shopkeepers. We found a bakery where I ventured into the rear, and after watching the bakers while they made up some French-type bread, I got carried away. Much to the delight of everyone, I joined the bakers on the bench to help them make up the day's supply.

We returned to the *Cuhona* laden with food and sundries in the island's fanciest transportation, a gilded horse-drawn carriage. The carriage itself was black with liberal dashes of vermilion, adorned with brightly polished silver headlamps, grab rails, steps, and dashing silver strips. It was truly a vintage Grecian hot rod.

The horse was another matter. It could hardly stand up. Fortunately, we took the route by the sea wall until we came to a hill, on the other side of which was our boat. The horse didn't make the hill. We climbed out and with a be-kind-to-animals feeling, walked the last half mile.

Tony organized his crew for the picture session and briefed us on what to expect, and seven of us left for the mansion of Baroness Roxana de Hurter. We climbed to the top of a hill that overlooked the town and had a panoramic view of blue ocean sprinkled with rugged, village-covered islands. It reminded me of the vistas of the Virgin Islands, only the weather seemed milder and less humid.

The house was a rebuilt home formerly owned by a wealthy Greek merchant. It had been modernized to the extent that an indoor bathroom, electricity, and a modern kitchen had been added. It was remodeled to the extent that more windows had been installed in some of the bedrooms, and the former stable had been converted to a beautiful, simple, but very effective living room. One end of the living room was set off by a sunken seating area that radiated around a fireplace.

Roxana, as she asked to be called, was a truly gracious lady whose hospitality knew no bounds. She greeted us at the patio gate with a warmth that made us feel as though we were meeting an old friend. Before giving us a conducted tour of her palace, we were taken to the living room, where Turkish coffee was served to those who wanted it and lemonade was available for the younger set.

Tony hovered unobtrusively in the background, shooting pictures of Roxanne, Lucy, Robin, and Chris. Every once in a while, I managed to stick my ugly bearded face in front of the lens.

We seemed to click right off with this wonderful woman, and since we didn't want to wear out our welcome, we invited her to walk back to the *Cuhona* with us so we could take her to one of the outlying islands for a swim.

She enthusiastically welcomed the invitation, but insisted that we first go to town so she could buy Robin some Green worry beads.

With beads in her tight fist, the rigors of the camera behind her, Robin happily led the gang back to the *Cuhona*. We were under way in jig time and headed for an island about thirty minutes' running time from Spetsai.

We pulled into a blue lagoon that was all but completely landlocked. To one side of this cove Roxanne pointed out some land that Liz Taylor and Richard Burton had recently acquired. The rest of the area was dotted with modern beach and summer homes.

I inquired about land costs, and after hearing Roxanne give the history of land values, I realized once again that I had come with too little too late.

Swimming was great. The water was the temperature of a tepid tub, yet it was inviting and invigorating. We had a small problem with jellyfish but became adept at swimming between the floating masses. These were not the man-o-war type that had long stringy stingers; these brown blobs were relatively docile and didn't sting unless one ran into direct contact with their underside. Fortunately, none of us had this experience, so we cannot report firsthand the consequences of such an encounter.

We impressed our delightful Roxanne with the spread that covered our luncheon table. I think that lunch was one of our most successful.

We had put what was left of Tony's barbecued lamb in a soup pot and for two days had been adding goodies to make a pasta lamb soup. Everyone must have enjoyed the repast, because they cleaned the pot, their plates, and the scraps on the table.

Unhappily, we had to leave our fine friend at Spetsai because we had to deliver Tom back to Athens. He was to return to the States, where he was going to meet his Chicago-based family, as well as visit the campus at Northwestern University.

We bid our farewells to Roxanne, and with a calm, dark blue sea, slightly rippled by a gentle easterly breeze, made our way back to Piraeus. We snoozed and read, and a few of us did some literary work in the form of letters, editorial writing for a magazine of the good life, *Look*, and, in my case, writing this forthcoming best seller.

At sunset our work was interrupted by the damnedest bleating of horns—it sounded like a traffic jam in Times Square on New Year's Eve. We all jumped out of our skins, running to the rail. Whoosh! The hydrofoil from Spetsai passed in a flash. The horns were their friendly greeting.

That interruption banished all our good and the rest of the time was spent discussing what, where, when, and how we were dining that evening. Everyone was heard from, even Robin, who suggested we all take our blankets wherever we went. Tony suggested a restaurant that was famous for a great long list of foods. He described some of the dishes with such appeal that we decided, almost unanimously, to give it a try. Those who didn't vote in the affirmative, as in any democratic society, got left on the boat. Maybe they were the smart ones.

We arrived at the restaurant, the Vassilenas Taverna, about 8:00 p.m. on that balmy evening with a bright, star-studded sky. We were escorted to a rooftop dining room so we could enjoy the wonders of nature while eating.

The waiter asked if we wanted full portions for everyone, including the six youngsters. Of course we wanted full portions; after all, everyone professed utter hunger. From then on we were in the hands of the waiters and the chef. The food just never stopped coming. Each dish was almost a meal in itself.

We had the following, served in this order:

1. Oysters
2. Olives
3. Green salad
4. Blue cheese paté
5. Tamara salad
6. Clams
7. Smoked sardines in olive oil
8. Shrimp in mayonnaise and mustard
9. Lamb gelatin
10. Stuffed vine leaves
11. Octopus
12. Fried mullet
13. Sauté of scampi
14. Retjina
15. Small squid sauté
16. Baby frankfurters
17. Meat rolled in fine pastry shells
18. Fried red mullet
19. Fish soup with safran
20. Steamed and roasted chicken
21. Watermelon
22. Cantaloupe

We didn't eat all the dinner. The following is what we gave up:

Roast lamb
Shish kebab
Pepper steak
Fried chicken legs
And for dessert, baklava.

I made it through almost every dish, although I admit that at the end I was tasting only a morsel. Ultimately, it became a divine kind of self-inflicted torture. I just had to try some more, even though I was so full that I felt like a three-hundred-pound blob.

Some were smarter than me. They gave up somewhere around courses fifteen or eighteen and quietly put their heads on the table and went to sleep. This act of surrender didn't faze the waiters one bit. They kept hauling in the food. It was quarter to twelve before we waddled from the table. Some had to carry or push others. That was a feast to fill a Roman, and the total cost was three dollars per person.

If I had to do it again, I would not eat so much in the beginning. I sort of shot my wad before the meal really got under way. I recommend that everyone have this experience at least once. For that matter, I wouldn't mind at all doing it again.

We managed to return to the boat, bloated and overstuffed, by hiring three taxis. We had fit into two on our way to the orgy. I, for one, took a whole bottle of gut fixer before retiring and slept like a log.

Saturday, Sunday, and Monday, September 3, 4, 5, 1966

The next three days were sort of jumbled into a mass of hurried visits to out-of-the-way harbors, small villages, and strolls through unspoiled countryside. We spent a good deal of time letting Tony take pictures by the hundreds. Len and Jackie and their two children made good company, especially in view of the crowded conditions we imposed on them. Chris, Luke, and I spent a good deal of time with Len giving him background for the prose portion of his future masterpiece on the carefree, irresponsible spend-it-by-the-jugful Burnses.

We spent some time in the city of Poros, which hadn't yet felt the impact of outside tourism. There seemed to be many native Greek visitors there, a number of good restaurants that catered strictly to Greek tastes, and innumerable curio shops cluttered with typical tourist trash. It was fun for us, because we were as much a curiosity to them as they were to our group.

Our shopping efforts became hilarious. The shopkeepers would try to peddle their worst goods at their highest prices to us. We, having been trained in Yugoslavia, were adept at saying no with gesticulating fervor. At the drop of a hat we could now feign indignant rage, shiver with frustration, and become red faced while spouting unintelligible nothings.

We surprised ourselves with the effectiveness of our dramatics. Prices came down and top-quality goods appeared from under counters and behind covered stacks. We were now giving easily less than we had before and getting much more.

Our meals took on the aura and taste of the Cordon Bleu. Luke had been demoted to assistant chef when Tony assumed total responsibility for the food preparation. I was banned from the cuisine entirely and therefore could criticize with impartial abandon. Grudgingly I had to admit that all the dishes that emanated from my former domain were above fault; as a matter of fact we had served to us such delicacies as tender fried calamari (squid), tarmara salada (farina, caviar, olive oil), spaghetti and noodles of many varieties, beautifully broiled octopus, and more pastas than I had ever eaten before—but that were great!

The highlight of our last days came about when, as cruise director, I issued an order saying that anyone wishing to eat on our last night out had to attend a predinner cocktail party in a costume of their own choosing.

Immediately upon reading the notice that I'd posted, the entire crew broke up into secretive groups of twos and threes to plan their costumes. As a special incentive there were to be prizes awarded for the best costumes in five categories. The award possibilities turned everyone on. Actually, no one spoke to anyone, except maybe to their particular partner in crime, for fear of spilling the beans about their proposed costume. As the cocktail hour approached, the air became electric with anticipation. A half hour before the appointed time, everyone seemed to assemble on the afterdeck, looking at but not speaking to one another. We were waiting for the other guy to make the first move to put his costume on.

I finally had to announce that anyone not in costume in twenty minutes would be banned from the boat. That announcement scattered them into feverish preparation, and the results were fabulous.

The winners of the five categories were as follows:

Robin—A special prize for coming in an old T-shirt as a baby beatnik
Geoff—The funniest, as a Greeknik
Linden—The prettiest as a harem girl
Lonnie—The most original as Tony Vaccaro
Chris—The scariest, as Medusa
Patti—The grand prize, as a Ubangi dancing girl complete with the exception of bare breasts

99

Other costumes worth special note were the captain, as a pirate; Pete as "Polly" Apollo; Julie, as her departed beau, Tom; Laurie as a Turkish street walker; Wendi, as a Turkish street walker's friend; Luke, as Robin with blanket; Tony, as an ancient Greek portrait painter; Len, as a wilted Mercury with singed wings; and finally myself, as Hafassus, the half-dressed, half-shaved, half-assed Roman.

We all laughed until the tears ran freely down our faces and our stomach muscles hurt with pleasure. The party was a great success and, I thought, a fitting climax to seven weeks aboard the *Cuhona*.

Upon our return to Piraeus, after visiting Poros and a few unnamed, unspoiled, and almost uninhabited small islands, our shipmates began to scatter to the four winds.

Pete gathered his gear and departed to spend a few days at the home of some of his Greek friends. The Grosses left en masse to spend a night cleaning up at the Athens Hilton before trekking back to de Gaulle-Land. Tony, after taking some final shots of his now dingy, wrinkled, yet still smiling subjects, headed for Rome.

Chris Miller, after sleeping for eighteen hours straight in preparation for her long flight home, boarded TWA for New York.

This left us with practically an empty boat. There were only eight Burnses, Chris Carl, and the crew. It was quiet—and kind of lonely.

As a last fling in the land of the ancients, the remainder of the once large and vigorous *Cuhona* crew dined at a quay-side restaurant in the old section of the port of Piraeus. Nostalgically, we sampled all our favorites so as to savor every taste as a fond and fitting reminder of a dream that came true.

Tuesday, September 6, 1966

We boarded BEA flight 153 at Athens airport for our flight to Geneva and back to a familiar civilization and more ordinary way of life.

This trip to Switzerland was our first gradual step back to reality. We still had four weeks before returning to California, but we felt that this could be best spent acclimatizing the four expatriates to be in their new environs. More important, three started with French lessons and Julie started in school.

We were on the road to home, happy, slightly heavier, and loaded with experiences enough to last most people a lifetime. I must admit, however, that in our case the events of the previous month and a half just served to whet our appetites.

"Now let's see . . . ," I said. "If we sold *Little Revenge* and got a fabulous price for it, we could then buy a Baglietto or that sixty-five-foot Benetti we saw in Trieste, take delivery in Barcelona, and . . ."

"Hey, Don," Luke gently reminded me, "what are we going to use for money?"

###################

www.ingramcontent.com/pod-product-compliance
Lightning Source LLC
Chambersburg PA
CBHW031243280526
45784CB00004B/1691